THE
Southern Living ®
COMPLETE
Do·Ahead
COOKBOOK

THE
Southern Living®
COMPLETE
Do·Ahead
COOKBOOK

Oxmoor House®

Cooking Ahead

Cooking ahead is neither a technique nor a style of preparation, but a way of life. It frees you to cook the dishes you want to when time is available.

The keys to cooking ahead are knowing which foods keep well, how long they will keep, and how to store and serve them. You'll find this critical information in over 300 recipes and 27 menus in *The Southern Living Complete Do-Ahead Cookbook*. Following these recipes and menus will bring many rewards. You will have a hearty main dish on hand when your family is hungry, a cake in the freezer when company drops by, a surprise to pack in your child's lunchbox, enough hors d'oeuvres to feed the small army of guests you invited to a party—foods that ensure good meals and good times. And depending on your schedule, many of the recipes offer refrigerating instructions and freezing instructions. Just choose the storage method that best suits your preparation schedule.

Cooking ahead is as old-fashioned as freezing your family's favorite casserole or simmering enough soup to last two or three days. And it's as up-to-date as the latest kitchen gadget that will help you whiz through preparing a second batch of your favorite recipe. Cooking ahead has always promised the economy and good nutrition of saving what's abundant for another day, and for today's household, the savings may be multiplied by having good food at home instead of dining out.

There's nothing very technical in this book—no laborious canning instructions or split-second microwave timing. There is just enough flexibility in choosing the time you will cook to make preparing and sharing wonderful food an enjoyable part of your busy life.

*Come home from work and take
made-ahead Spaghetti and Meatballs
and Italian Vegetable Salad from the
refrigerator for a family treat. Menu
begins on page 176.*

Finding the Time

Freezing and refrigeration have expanded the possibilities of make-ahead cooking to include at least part of almost any recipe. What you will find in *The Southern Living Complete Do-Ahead Cookbook* are those foods that can be refrigerated, frozen, or kept at room temperature for periods of time ranging from overnight to 1 year without loss of flavor or texture, and with minimal reduction of nutrients. This means that you don't have to find time to cook just before mealtime. If a recipe indicates that a dish can be frozen up to one month, then you can prepare it anytime up to one month before serving.

But finding time to clean and cook vegetables for a soup or to measure and mix the ingredients for a cake can be difficult for many cooks. To resolve this problem, you can break down procedures into smaller time spans. You can clean the vegetables one day, and cook the soup the next. You can measure ingredients for a cake several days before baking the cake as long as you refrigerate the perishables and store the dry ingredients in airtight containers.

Cooking time does not have to be continuous. If you are making a spaghetti sauce, you can start the sauce, cook it for an hour, cool it slightly, and refrigerate it in a tightly covered container. Later that day or the next, reheat the sauce to simmering and complete the cooking. This holds true for any simmered food, such as a soup or stew, that requires more than an hour on the stove. Just be sure that any meat or poultry in the dish is cooked thoroughly before you remove the pot from the heat—there shouldn't be any pinkness.

If you're chopping onions, green pepper, or parsley, you can just as easily chop enough for two recipes; divide the chopped vegetables, and refrigerate or freeze part of them for use in another dish. (Chopped onion should be used within a month.)

Doubling a recipe can be the most straightforward time-saver. In many recipes you can double the ingredients and divide them into two batches. If you decide to put twice the amount of food into one pot, as with a soup or stew, you'll need a pot large enough so that foods will brown quickly and liquids can simmer without boiling over. The larger quantity of food will probably take longer to cook, so you will have to rely on signs of doneness rather than timing.

While the food processor is out, chop an extra batch of peppers and onions to keep on hand in the freezer.

Helpful Equipment

Be prepared to cook ahead by planning your shopping ahead. Failing to do this may result in your "found" time being spent in the supermarket instead of in the kitchen.

A separate chest-type or upright freezer may encourage make-ahead cooking, but the freezer attached to your refrigerator can hold many meals. Temperature, however, is critical. Maximum storage times, according to the Freezer Guide on page 230, are for foods kept at 0°F or lower. If the temperature in your freezer is 10°F, count on only half the storage time. A separate freezer will generally stay colder because it is opened less frequently than one attached to a refrigerator. In either, a freezer thermometer will let you know whether prolonged storage is feasible in your freezer.

Some more puzzling questions most cooks face are what's in the freezer and how long has it been there. The value of the freezer is limited if the food in it has not been labeled and dated. And the value of even a small refrigerator/freezer will be greatly enhanced if you keep a list of its contents and the date the foods were placed in the freezer. For maximum convenience, include a list of any ingredients that are needed to complete, garnish, or accompany each prepared dish so that you can have these items on hand before you defrost the frozen item. If the recipe is in this cookbook, include the page number on the label so that you can quickly turn to the instructions for reheating and serving.

The microwave oven, when used in conjunction with the freezer, is often mentioned as a cook's greatest convenience. You can freeze a whole dish or single portions and defrost and reheat the food in minutes in the microwave oven. Cookware designed to go from freezer to microwave to table minimizes clean-up time. The microwave oven makes it possible to defrost and reheat meals when needed. And it gives you greater cook-ahead flexibility for defrosting and heating ingredients kept in the freezer.

Be sure to note on the label the number of servings as well as any ingredients that need to be added to the frozen item once it is thawed.

Entire meals frozen in labeled individual microwave-safe trays make it easy for family members to help themselves to dinner.

A blender, automatic rice cooker, food processor, salad spinner, mini-chopper, or ice cream freezer can add convenience to daily kitchen routines.

Any appliance that offers a shortcut will make cooking ahead more convenient. Some equipment you may want to consider:

Food Processor   The larger food processors make it possible to process a double batch of ingredients without emptying the processor bowl. It can be especially useful for making large batches of chopped meat mixtures and bread dough. Whatever size food processor you may have, an extra processor bowl or two can make the work go much faster. You can switch bowls instead of emptying and cleaning the bowl between steps, or you can prepare ingredients for more than one recipe at a time.

Mini-Chopper   A pint-size chopper makes quick work of mincing a single clove of garlic or a few fresh herbs. It also provides you with a second chopping tool so that you can be preparing one ingredient in the food processor and another in the mini-chopper. And most mini-choppers are easier to clean.

Salad Spinner   Washing lettuce and parsley when you bring them home from the store or whenever you have a spare moment is an uncomplicated do-ahead task. Wrap the freshly washed and dried greens in paper towels and place in a zip-top plastic bag. They will keep in the vegetable bin of the refrigerator about a week.

Electric or Hand-Turned Ice Cream Freezer   This piece of equipment isn't essential, of course. But homemade ice cream, sorbet, and frozen yogurt keep well, and they can turn ripe seasonal fruits into a make-ahead bounty.

Automatic Cookers Some cooks swear by slow cookers, especially for stews and pot roasts, because you can prepare food in the morning and come home to a cooked main dish at night. Cherished in Oriental kitchens, automatic rice cookers not only cook rice perfectly every time but also halt the cooking and keep the rice warm, making the timing flexible. In addition, they make it possible to cook large quantities of rice at one time so that you will have some left over for use in another recipe.

Storing Prepared Foods _____

Each recipe in this book has specific instructions for proper storage. The key to keeping foods fresh is to seal out air, so use containers with tight-fitting lids and heavy-duty zip-top plastic bags, plastic wrap, or aluminum foil.

Foods to be frozen, except baked goods that must cool to room temperature, should be refrigerated first, so that they are cooler when you put them in the freezer. Foods will freeze faster if they start out at a lower temperature, and the faster the food freezes, the fresher it will taste when reheated and served. Food also freezes faster in smaller quantities, but the smaller amounts leave more surface area exposed to the slow oxidation that causes frozen food to deteriorate. So consider your own convenience; you'll probably want to freeze some items in individual portions and others in family-size amounts. Do not refreeze cooked dishes that have been frozen and reheated once before; flavor and nutrients will suffer, and there is increased danger of bacterial growth.

Glass or rigid plastic containers with tight-fitting lids are perfect for freezing casseroles, soups, and baked items.

For the butcher wrap, place food diagonally in one corner of freezer wrap. Fold the corner over the food. Then fold sides in tightly, and roll up. Seal and label the package.

For the drugstore wrap, place food in center of freezer wrap. Bring the short ends together and fold down. Then fold sides to form points; press points under package. Seal and label the package.

Wrap all foods to minimize exposure to air and moisture. Do not use ordinary plastic wrap and aluminum foil, thin plastic bags, and dairy cartons in the freezer. Safeguard your investment of time and money by storing foods in containers and wrappings designed for the freezer. These will be labeled as such when you buy them. They fall into three general categories:

Rigid Containers   These may be plastic, plastic-coated cardboard, or glass. They are excellent for liquids and may be used for all but irregularly shaped foods, such as a whole chicken or a roll of cookie dough. Their own lids, used with freezer tape, if directed, provide an adequate seal. Choose a container not much larger than the food it will hold, but do leave about one inch of space between the level of the food and the top of the container, because liquids and the moisture in solid foods will expand as they freeze. Choose microwave-safe containers for convenient microwave defrosting and reheating.

Freezer Wraps   Use heavy-duty aluminum foil and plastic-coated freezer paper for wrapping odd-shaped items. Some plastic wraps are sturdy enough for freezer use; check the label to be sure. You'll need freezer tape to secure wrappings; ordinary tape will loosen in the freezer. If you are stacking several items in one package, such as meat patties, chops, or cutlets, separate them with double layers of wax paper, plastic wrap, or freezer paper. To wrap food effectively, use either the butcher wrap, or the drugstore wrap method for wrapping food with freezer paper.

Freezer Bags   Use only those plastic bags labeled for freezer use. After you have put the food in the bag, press out as much air as possible before sealing and labeling. If you freeze large quantities of food as well as prepared dishes, you may want to invest in a vacuum-seal appliance that cuts bags from a roll to fit foods and provides an airtight seal. An advantage of this system is that you can

Line a baking dish with heavy-duty aluminum foil, leaving a generous overhang. Add food and freeze until firm enough to remove from the dish.

When frozen, remove food from the dish. Fold overhangs to seal; label food and return to the freezer. This allows the dish to be used for other recipes.

boil the food in the bag to reheat—a time-saver if you don't have a microwave oven.

Good freezer packaging should protect the food as well as give you easy access to the items in desired quantities. Here are some ways to package prepared dishes for convenient reheating and serving:

Aluminum Foil Pans   Baked foods such as lasagna and meat loaf can be baked, frozen, and reheated in the same heavy-duty aluminum foil pan. Freeze the dish, cooked or uncooked, and wrap it tightly with heavy-duty aluminum foil or freezer paper. Aluminum foil pans can be washed and reused if they haven't been damaged.

Lined Baking Dishes   If you don't want to leave a dish in the freezer, line the dish with heavy-duty aluminum foil or plastic wrap, leaving a generous overhang on all four sides of the dish. Add the food, and freeze until solid. Remove the foil liner, and wrap the food, using the foil or plastic wrap overhangs, or seal it in a freezer bag. Label the food package, and return it to the freezer. When ready to serve, remove all wrapping, and replace the food in the dish to reheat.

Single Servings   Freeze single servings of soup, stew, chili, and spaghetti sauce in individual microwave-safe containers or freezer bags for fast help-yourself convenience. If you don't have a lot of small containers or don't want them cluttering your freezer, freeze portions of food in bowls, mugs, or giant-size muffin tins lined with plastic wrap. Place the containers on a baking sheet to hold them steady in the freezer. After the food is frozen, wrap the single portions with plastic wrap, and toss them into a freezer bag. Remove the plastic wrap before microwaving.

Tray Meals   Making complete meals for reheating in a conventional oven is tricky, because cooking times must be coordinated so that one food doesn't overcook before another is heated through. Commercial frozen food packagers address this problem by pre-cooking the parts of a dinner to varying degrees of doneness. You will achieve better results with tray dinners if you include only meats and grains; cook vegetables separately just before serving time for best flavor, texture, and nutrient retention.

Tray combinations are easier to coordinate if using microwave ovens because everything heats quickly and will stay moist if covered with plastic wrap or the plastic lid that comes with the dish. To prepare for freezing, arrange the meal's main course and accompaniments on divided microwave-safe plastic or heavy paper plates. Freeze plates on baking sheets; remove from freezer, and wrap tightly in freezer plastic wrap, or wrap in regular plastic wrap, and place in large freezer bags. Do not include bread or desserts with the meal because they reheat much faster than meats, grains, and vegetables.

From Storage to Table _____

Most cooked foods do not have to be defrosted before baking or reheating. You can take most foods out of the freezer and put them in the refrigerator about eight hours before you plan to serve them. Do not defrost at room temperature dishes that contain meat, fish, eggs, or poultry. You will find specific instructions for reheating and serving with each recipe in this book. Below are general procedures for reheating.

Stovetop Reheating   Frozen soups, sauces, and stews can be reheated on the stovetop without defrosting. To prevent scorching, start cooking over low heat, and add just enough water to cover the bottom of the pan, or use a double boiler. Stir often to break up the food and distribute heat evenly.

When the food has defrosted, you can increase the heat to medium. Cook and stir until soups just reach the boiling point; cover stews, sauces, and other semi-liquid foods, and simmer about five minutes or until thoroughly heated. If the food has thickened or lost some of its moisture, stir in some water while reheating. Ingredients such as lemon juice, vinegar, and fresh herbs lose some of their strength during storage and reheating. However, more seasonings can be added as desired during reheating.

Oven Reheating   A casserole will reheat faster and with less risk of dryness if it has been defrosted in the refrigerator. If there was no chance to defrost it, bake it in a moderate oven, allowing extra baking time. Use bubbling edges, brownness, and other signs of doneness as your guide to timing. Cover the dish if the food seems to be getting too dry. Add toppings after the food has defrosted, or the topping may burn before the food is done. Unbaked pies, pastries, and other crisp or crusty treats should not be defrosted before reheating. Follow specific recipe directions.

Microwave Reheating   Follow the directions in your microwave oven owner's manual. Small quantities of food heat more evenly in the microwave oven, so it makes sense to reheat individual portions on serving plates. Small quantities needn't be defrosted, but they should be stirred, if possible, to distribute heat evenly, and the plate should be covered unless the food has a crisp topping. Larger quantities of food should be defrosted on LOW (30% power) before reheating. Be careful not to reheat foods too long in the microwave oven. Check individual portions every minute and stir, if possible. Check larger quantities every two minutes, stirring, if possible. This will prevent overcooking and dryness.

Many of the recipes in this book include directions for adding a topping or a garnish when reheating or before serving. These quickly prepared items add a fresh taste and appearance to the dish. You can add a garnish to the recipes with sprinklings of chopped fresh parsley or other fresh herbs, extra grated Parmesan cheese, citrus slices, chopped tomatoes or sweet pepper, shredded carrot or radish, croutons, toasted almond slices, or chopped nuts or olives.

Make-Ahead Fare on the Menu _____

The natural choices to complement made-ahead dishes are those foods that should be prepared close to serving time for best nutrient retention, flavor, and texture. Most important among foods to prepare just before serving are fruits and vegetables; some of their precious vitamin content begins to diminish as soon as they are cut, and this process is hastened by cooking and storage. Among the four to six servings of fruits and vegetables that everyone should consume daily, it is wise to include at least one serving of raw fruit and a small green salad, because the uncooked produce provides nutrients and fiber that may be lost in cooking.

If you have a made-ahead entrée ready to reheat, then your cooking time before a meal should be spent preparing fresh produce—perhaps baking potatoes and cutting up crudités, steaming broccoli and arranging salads of lettuce and tomato, or boiling green beans and slicing a melon for dessert. None of this needs to be elaborate; the less you do to fresh foods apart from basic cooking, the more nutritious the dish is likely to be. The important place of grains on everyday menus can often be filled with good bakery breads, but pasta practically cooks itself, couscous can be done in five minutes, and you can steam rice, bulgur, or barley "automatically" with a rice cooker or with predictably good results in the microwave oven.

If you have a soup, stew, or casserole ready to reheat, you can set up a salad bar while the entrée is heating. Or, if you wish, you can bake potatoes and set up a "potato bar" with a selection of cheeses, bacon bits, chives, and other toppings. The same concept will work with cooked green vegetables, which can be matched with a choice of toasted nuts, breadcrumbs, chopped egg, pimiento, Parmesan cheese, or various seasoned butters, or salad dressings.

Impromptu Entertaining ————

Many cooks don't get too systematic about cooking ahead until they face a big party countdown. The only calm way to anticipate the arrival of 40 people for cocktails is to fill the refrigerator and freezer well in advance with plenty of appetizers and snacks. The only way to share a multi-course sit-down dinner—and enjoy the conversation with the six or eight friends you've invited—is to do most of the cooking ahead. You'll find several specific party menus in the chapter Ready for Entertaining. But every recipe in this book is well suited to some kind of party plan, whether a brunch, a picnic, a covered-dish supper, an open house, or a romantic dinner for two.

When you are composing a party menu, do keep in mind what kind of reheating or last-minute finishing touches each dish will need and in what kind of pan, pot, or dish. Try to coordinate recipes so that you won't have to bake more dishes at the last minute than your oven can hold—or need more baking sheets than you own or can borrow. Think about creating some "breathing time" for yourself at a sit-down dinner by including a cold or room temperature first course and dessert—perhaps ones that can be placed on the plates before guests are seated. And don't overlook recipes for beverages, breads, pickles, and relishes in any do-ahead menu; these foods can add distinction to a simple meal with the greatest of serving ease.

When your guest list is long or your dinner plan fancy, you'll want to select recipes that allow for a comfortable sequence of preparations and a viable storage plan. For greatest flexibility in time and space, choose some party fare that can be tucked into the freezer weeks ahead, some items that will hold in the refrigerator up to a week, and at least one item that will keep well for up to a week at room temperature, such as a snack mix.

Remember also that the invitation to share make-ahead fare needn't come from you. It can be a neighbor's suggestion that you drop by for coffee, a relative's expectation that you'll spend the weekend, your office holiday party, or any situation where a food gift would be appropriate. Many of the recipes in this book not only keep well but also wrap and travel well—and it is as wonderful to have them ready for giving as it is to have them ready to serve at home.

When You Have Time

Take just a few minutes to prepare seasoned butters and you can freeze taste treasures that will last for months. Devote half an hour to making a pie crust, and you'll be able to serve an impromptu dessert whenever unexpected guests arrive. Turn pick-of-the-crop produce into roasted peppers or freezer jam, and you'll enjoy a bountiful harvest year-round.

The recipes in this chapter are culinary building blocks that can be stored from one to 12 months. Prepare them when you have time, and they will be ready to incorporate into, or serve with, other foods. Not only are these foods more economical to make than they are to buy, but more important, you can't buy prepared foods as delicious as these. For everyday convenience try the easily made barbecue and spaghetti sauces, salad dressings, or herb vinegars in this chapter.

Discovering the versatility of these foods is part of the joy of having them on hand. Make three or four kinds of seasoned butters, and you will have instant enhancers for pasta, grilled fish and meats, baked potatoes, and steamed vegetables, or sweet toppings for toast, pancakes, and muffins. Roast garlic to blend with mayonnaise, and use it as a sauce for a cold chicken lunch or a dip for tomorrow night's party. Match roasted red, green, and yellow peppers with goat cheese or hard salami to create appetizers that will set an elegant tone for a special dinner—or heap the roasted peppers on a hero sandwich for a satisfying supper. Try the caramelized onions, and you won't believe how flavorful they can be when served over broiled or roasted meats or stirred into a rich French onion soup.

Toss a fresh salad anytime with delicious made-ahead toppings such as crisp Herbed Croutons (page 27) and Fresh French Dressing or Creamy Buttermilk Dressing (page 26).

Strawberry Freezer Jam

2 cups crushed fresh
  strawberries
4 cups sugar
1 (1¾-ounce) package powdered
  pectin
¾ cup water

Combine strawberries and sugar, stirring well. Let stand 20 minutes, stirring occasionally.

Combine pectin and water in a small saucepan. Bring to a boil; boil 1 minute, stirring constantly. Pour pectin mixture over strawberry mixture; stir 3 minutes. Immediately pour jam into jelly jars or frozen food containers, leaving ½-inch headspace. Cover at once with lids. Cool to room temperature.

TO STORE: Refrigerate jam up to 3 weeks. Freeze up to 1 year.

TO SERVE: Thaw at room temperature. Serve with biscuits, pancakes, or French toast or over ice cream or pound cake. Yield: 6 cups.

Strawberry Puree

2 cups fresh strawberries
¼ cup sugar
2 teaspoons amaretto or other
  almond-flavored liqueur

Combine all ingredients in container of an electric blender; process until smooth.

TO STORE: Refrigerate puree in a tightly covered container up to 2 weeks. Freeze puree in a labeled airtight container up to 3 months.

TO SERVE: Thaw puree in refrigerator, or defrost on MEDIUM LOW (30% power) in microwave oven. Serve puree over ice cream, angel food cake, or pound cake. Yield: 1½ cups.

Pineapple Puree: Substitute 2 cups fresh pineapple chunks for strawberries and 1 tablespoon dark rum and 1 teaspoon lime juice for amaretto. Serve over ice cream, angel food cake, or pound cake. Yield: 1½ cups.

Fresh Strawberry-Orange Butter

1 cup sliced fresh strawberries
1 cup unsalted butter or
  margarine, softened
¼ cup honey
1 tablespoon grated orange rind

Position knife blade in food processor bowl; add all ingredients. Process 1 minute or until fluffy, scraping sides of processor bowl once.

TO STORE: Refrigerate butter in a tightly covered container up to 2 weeks. Freeze butter in a labeled airtight container up to 6 months.

TO SERVE: Thaw in refrigerator. Serve with pancakes, French toast, biscuits, or muffins. Yield: 1¾ cups.

Cinnamon-Honey Butter

½ cup unsalted butter or
   margarine, softened
2 tablespoons honey
1 teaspoon ground cinnamon

Cream butter until light and fluffy. Add honey and cinnamon, beating until well blended. Place butter on wax paper, and shape into two 2½-inch sticks.

TO STORE: Cover tightly, and freeze up to 6 months.

TO SERVE: Thaw sticks in refrigerator; cut off pats as needed. Serve with pancakes, waffles, muffins, or toast. Yield: ½ cup.

Nut Butter: Add ¼ cup ground toasted pecans to creamed butter, beating well. Serve with rice or other cooked grains. Yield: ½ cup.

Orange Butter: Add ¼ cup sifted powdered sugar and 1 tablespoon grated orange rind to creamed butter, beating well. Serve with cooked vegetables such as carrots or sweet potatoes. Yield: ½ cup.

Chive Butter: Add ¼ cup minced fresh chives to creamed butter, beating well. Serve with broiled chicken, fish, pasta, or potatoes. Yield: ½ cup.

Garlic Butter: Add 2 tablespoons minced fresh parsley and 1 tablespoon crushed garlic to creamed butter, beating well. Serve with bread, broiled seafood, or cooked vegetables. Yield: ½ cup.

Chicken Broth

6 pounds chicken pieces
2½ quarts water
3 stalks celery with leaves, cut
   into 1-inch pieces
2 medium onions, quartered
1 bay leaf
1½ teaspoons salt
¾ teaspoon pepper
½ teaspoon dried whole thyme

Combine all ingredients in a large Dutch oven. Bring to a boil; cover, reduce heat, and simmer 1½ hours. Strain broth through a cheesecloth- or paper towel-lined sieve, reserving chicken pieces and vegetables for other uses. Cover broth, and chill thoroughly. Skim and discard solidified fat from top of broth.

TO STORE: Refrigerate broth in a tightly covered container up to 3 days. Freeze in a labeled airtight container up to 3 months.

TO SERVE: Thaw and use as directed in recipes that call for chicken broth. Yield: 10 cups.

Easy Barbecue Sauce is quick to make. When grilling or baking, brush it on beef, chicken, or pork for an extra touch of flavor.

Easy Barbecue Sauce

1 (16-ounce) can tomato sauce
1 cup chopped onion
½ cup Worcestershire sauce
¼ cup butter or margarine
¼ cup vegetable oil
2 tablespoons sugar
2 tablespoons dark brown sugar
2 teaspoons instant coffee
   granules
1 teaspoon salt
1 teaspoon garlic powder
1 teaspoon pepper
½ teaspoon ground ginger
½ teaspoon ground allspice

Combine all ingredients in a medium saucepan. Bring mixture to a boil; reduce heat, and simmer 10 minutes, stirring occasionally. Cool completely.

TO STORE: Refrigerate in a tightly covered container up to 1 month.

TO SERVE: Stir well. Brush on beef, pork, or chicken during grilling, broiling, or baking. Yield: 3½ cups.

Roasted Garlic Mayonnaise

12 cloves garlic
1 tablespoon vegetable oil
1 tablespoon fresh lemon juice
1 teaspoon Worcestershire sauce
1 cup mayonnaise
¼ cup chopped fresh parsley
¼ cup chopped fresh basil
Salt and pepper to taste

Place garlic and oil in a small baking dish; stir well. Bake at 300° for 30 minutes or until garlic is soft and golden. Cool to room temperature.

Place garlic mixture, lemon juice, and Worcestershire sauce in container of an electric blender; process until smooth. Add mayonnaise and remaining ingredients; process until smooth.

TO STORE: Refrigerate in a tightly covered container up to 1 month.

TO SERVE: Serve mayonnaise with grilled poultry, fish, or vegetables, or use as a dip for cold seafood or crudités. Yield: 1 cup.

Caramelized Onions

3 pounds onions (about 8 medium), thinly sliced
¼ cup plus 2 tablespoons butter, melted

Separate onions into rings; cook in butter in a large Dutch oven over low heat 3 hours or until onion is lightly browned, stirring once each hour for the first 2 hours, and every 15 minutes the last hour.

TO STORE: Refrigerate onions in a tightly covered container up to 1 week. Freeze in a labeled airtight container up to 6 months.

TO SERVE: Cook over low heat until hot, stirring occasionally. Serve with broiled or roasted meats or poultry, or use to prepare Easy French Onion Soup. Yield: about 2½ cups.

Easy French Onion Soup

2½ cups Caramelized Onions
2 (10½-ounce) cans condensed beef broth, undiluted
7 (¾-inch-thick) slices French bread
1 cup (4 ounces) shredded Gruyère cheese

Cook onions over low heat until hot, stirring occasionally. Add water to beef broth to equal 5 cups. Stir broth mixture into onions; cook over medium heat until thoroughly heated.

Place bread slices on a baking sheet; sprinkle evenly with cheese. Broil 6 inches from heat 2 to 3 minutes or until lightly browned.

Ladle soup into individual soup bowls; top each with a slice of French bread, cheese side up. Yield: 7 cups.

Roasted Peppers

12 medium-size sweet red,
    green, or yellow peppers
Olive or vegetable oil

Wash and dry peppers. Cut peppers in half lengthwise; remove seeds. Place half of peppers, skin side up, on a lightly greased baking sheet. Broil 6 inches from heat 5 to 10 minutes or until skins are charred. Place peppers in a plastic bag; close tightly, and let stand 10 minutes to loosen skins. Peel peppers, and cut into ½-inch strips. Repeat procedure with remaining peppers. Place peppers in an airtight container; add just enough oil to cover peppers.

TO STORE: Refrigerate up to 1 month, adding oil, if needed, to keep peppers covered.

TO SERVE: Remove peppers from oil; drain off excess oil. Serve peppers with sautéed sausage, veal, or chicken or as an accompaniment to fresh mozzarella or goat cheese. Roasted Peppers may also be used to prepare Tomato Pepper Sauce. Yield: 4 cups.

Note: Roasted Peppers may be pureed and frozen in airtight containers without oil up to 3 months.

Tomato Pepper Sauce

⅔ cup Roasted Peppers
2 tablespoons olive oil
1 cup peeled, seeded, and
    chopped tomato
1 tablespoon capers
1 tablespoon chopped fresh
    parsley
1 tablespoon chopped fresh
    cilantro
¼ teaspoon salt

Place peppers in container of an electric blender; process until smooth.
Heat oil in a medium saucepan. Stir in pureed peppers, tomato, and remaining ingredients; reduce heat, and simmer 5 minutes. Serve with grilled chicken or fish. Yield: 1¾ cups.

Strawberry Vinegar

2 cups sliced fresh strawberries
2 cups white wine vinegar
¼ cup sugar

Place strawberries in a 1-quart jar. Press strawberries with a wooden spoon to release juice; set aside. Combine vinegar and sugar in a medium saucepan. Bring to a boil; reduce heat, and simmer until sugar dissolves. Pour vinegar mixture over strawberries; cover with airtight lid. Let stand at room temperature 48 hours. Strain vinegar through a cheesecloth- or paper towel-lined sieve; discard strawberries.
Place vinegar in a medium saucepan. Bring to a boil; boil 2 minutes. Cool; pour into 2 half-pint jars.

TO STORE: Store at room temperature indefinitely.

TO SERVE: Use in salad dressings or vinaigrettes. Yield: 2 cups.

Basil Vinegar

1 cup packed fresh basil leaves
1 quart red or white wine
    vinegar
Fresh basil sprigs
2 cloves garlic, halved

Slightly bruise 1 cup basil leaves; place in a 1-quart jar. Bring vinegar to a boil in a medium saucepan; pour over basil leaves. Cover with airtight lid, and store in a dark place 2 to 4 weeks.

Strain vinegar into decorative jars, discarding basil leaves. Add basil sprigs and garlic. Seal jars with cork or other airtight lid.

TO STORE: Store at room temperature indefinitely.

TO SERVE: Use in salad dressings, vinaigrettes, or basting sauces. Yield: 3¾ cups.

Tarragon-Lemon Vinegar: Substitute fresh tarragon for basil leaves. After straining, add fresh tarragon sprigs and lemon rind spirals. Yield: 3¾ cups.

Turn ordinary salad dressings and vinaigrettes into something special with Basil or Tarragon-Lemon Vinegar. Store the vinegars in decorative bottles.

Creamy Buttermilk Dressing

1 cup mayonnaise
1 cup buttermilk
¼ cup minced fresh chives
2 tablespoons minced fresh
  parsley
1 clove garlic, crushed
¼ teaspoon salt
⅛ teaspoon ground white
  pepper

Combine all ingredients in a small bowl; stir well.

TO STORE: Refrigerate in a tightly covered container at least 2 hours and up to 2 weeks.

TO SERVE: Stir well before serving. Serve over salad, or use to prepare Bacon-Buttermilk Dressing. Yield: 2 cups.

Bacon-Buttermilk Dressing: Stir 7 slices of cooked and crumbled bacon into Creamy Buttermilk Dressing. Yield: 2¼ cups.

Fresh French Dressing

1 cup vegetable oil
⅓ cup catsup
¼ cup sugar
¼ cup finely chopped onion
¼ cup cider vinegar
1 teaspoon celery seeds
Salt to taste

Combine all ingredients in container of an electric blender; process until smooth.

TO STORE: Refrigerate in a tightly covered container at least 2 hours and up to 2 weeks.

TO SERVE: Stir well before serving. Serve over salad, or use to prepare Russian Dressing. Yield: 1½ cups.

Russian Dressing

1 cup mayonnaise
½ cup Fresh French Dressing
2 tablespoons minced onion
2 tablespoons minced green
  pepper
2 tablespoons minced pimiento
2 teaspoons prepared
  horseradish

Combine all ingredients in a small bowl, stirring well. Yield: 1¾ cups.

Vinaigrette Dressing

¾ cup vegetable oil
¼ cup red wine vinegar
1 clove garlic, crushed
¼ teaspoon salt
¼ teaspoon freshly ground
  pepper

Combine all ingredients in a jar. Cover tightly, and shake vigorously.

TO STORE: Refrigerate up to 1 month.

TO SERVE: Shake dressing well. Serve as a salad dressing, or use as a marinade for meats, seafood, or vegetables. Yield: 1 cup.

Croutons

6 slices French bread, crust
   removed
¼ cup butter or margarine

Cut bread slices into ½-inch cubes. Melt butter in a large skillet; add bread cubes, and toss to coat. Spread bread cubes on an ungreased baking sheet. Bake at 300° for 30 minutes or until very crisp, stirring every 5 minutes. Cool completely.

TO STORE: Store croutons in an airtight container at room temperature up to 1 week. Freeze in a labeled airtight container up to 1 month.

TO SERVE: Serve croutons with soups or salads. Yield: about 2 cups.

Herbed Croutons: Add 1 teaspoon dried whole oregano, 1 teaspoon dried whole basil, and ½ teaspoon garlic powder to melted butter; toss with bread cubes. Yield: about 2 cups.

Pastry Shell

1 cup all-purpose flour
¼ teaspoon salt
3 tablespoons shortening
2 tablespoons cold butter
2 to 3 tablespoons cold water

Combine flour and salt; cut in shortening and butter with a pastry blender until mixture resembles coarse meal. Sprinkle cold water (1 tablespoon at a time) evenly over surface; stir with a fork until dry ingredients are moistened. Shape pastry into a ball; chill.
Roll pastry to ⅛-inch thickness on a lightly floured surface. Place in a 9-inch pieplate; trim off excess pastry along edges. Fold edges under and flute.

TO STORE: Cover tightly, and freeze up to 6 months.

TO SERVE: For baked pastry shell, thaw slightly, and prick bottom and sides of pastry shell generously with a fork. Bake at 450° for 12 to 14 minutes or until pastry shell is golden brown. For filled pies, thaw pastry shell, and follow directions in specific recipes. Yield: one 9-inch pastry shell.

Chocolate Crumb Crust

1½ cups chocolate wafer
   crumbs
⅓ cup butter or margarine,
   melted

Combine crumbs and butter in a small bowl; stir well. Firmly press crumb mixture evenly over bottom and up the sides of a 9-inch pieplate. Bake at 350° for 8 minutes. Cool completely.

TO STORE: Cover tightly, and freeze up to 6 months.

TO SERVE: Fill frozen crust with desired filling. Yield: one 9-inch crust.

Ground Beef Mix

3 pounds ground beef
1 large green pepper, finely
   chopped
3 cloves garlic, minced
1 cup water
1 tablespoon plus 1 teaspoon
   beef-flavored bouillon granules
2 medium onions, finely
   chopped
¼ teaspoon pepper

Combine beef, green pepper, and garlic in a large skillet. Cook over medium-high heat until meat is browned, stirring to crumble meat; drain well. Remove meat from skillet. Add water and bouillon granules to skillet. Bring to a boil, stirring to dissolve granules. Add onion; cover, reduce heat to medium, and cook 15 minutes. Uncover and cook 5 to 10 minutes or until liquid evaporates. Stir onion mixture and pepper into beef mixture.

TO STORE: Spread beef mixture in a 15- x 10- x 1-inch jellyroll pan; cool. Cover tightly, and freeze at least 4 hours. Crumble frozen mixture into small pieces. Freeze in a labeled airtight container up to 2 months.

TO SERVE: Use in Quick Chili or Quick Meaty Spaghetti Sauce. Yield: 10 cups.

Quick Chili

3⅓ cups Ground Beef Mix
1 (15½-ounce) can red kidney
   beans, undrained
1 (14½-ounce) can whole
   tomatoes, undrained and
   chopped
2 teaspoons chili powder
½ teaspoon dried whole
   oregano
½ teaspoon ground cumin
½ teaspoon ground coriander
½ teaspoon salt
¼ teaspoon pepper

Cook frozen Ground Beef Mix in a 3-quart saucepan over medium heat until thoroughly heated. Add beans and remaining ingredients; stir well. Bring mixture to a boil; reduce heat, and simmer, uncovered, 15 to 20 minutes, stirring occasionally. Yield: 5 cups.

Quick Spaghetti Sauce

3⅓ cups Ground Beef Mix
1 (28-ounce) can crushed
   tomatoes
½ cup water
¼ cup tomato paste
¼ cup chopped fresh parsley
1 bay leaf
½ teaspoon dried whole basil
½ teaspoon dried whole
   oregano
¼ to ½ teaspoon salt
¼ teaspoon dried whole thyme
¼ teaspoon pepper
Hot cooked spaghetti

Cook frozen Ground Beef Mix in a 3-quart saucepan over medium heat until thoroughly heated. Add crushed tomatoes and next 9 ingredients; stir well. Bring mixture to a boil; reduce heat, and simmer 20 minutes, stirring occasionally. Remove and discard bay leaf. Serve sauce over hot cooked spaghetti. Yield: 6 cups.

Top spaghetti with Quick Spaghetti Sauce for a hearty dinner to warm up a cold winter evening.

No·Rush Breakfast and Brunch

Maybe the best thing about a made-ahead breakfast is that you don't have to worry about preparing it when you wake up. Or maybe the best thing is the smell of muffins in the oven while the coffee is still brewing. Or maybe it's feeling relaxed about serving brunch to several guests.

More than any other meal, breakfast is a personal matter. Make-ahead recipes can satisfy individual preferences such as an eat-in-the-car granola bar or a quick bowl of nourishing homemade cereal and fruit. Those who like to linger over breakfast can choose French toast, grits and sausage, or a hash brown casserole.

When breakfast becomes brunch, make-ahead foods can still give you more slumber time. Welcome guests with mixed-ahead orange-cranberry coolers or mugfuls of rich coffee punch. The main course may include frozen-ahead cornbread cakes topped with rich creamed ham, delicate cream puffs retrieved from the freezer and filled with a freshly scrambled egg mixture, or a ham and broccoli casserole assembled the night before.

It suits the hour to keep things simple. The casseroles were selected because overnight refrigeration gives flavors time to mingle. The batters for muffins and pancakes can be refrigerated up to a week. Creamed ham freezes well, as do turkey sausage patties for the English muffin sandwiches. The breakfast cereal is good enough to serve as a snack, and the granola bars probably would keep for weeks in the pantry if they weren't eaten so fast!

Light and fluffy Refrigerator Buttermilk Pancakes (page 35) allow you to sleep in and still enjoy a satisfying breakfast. Stack pancakes high and top them with fresh fruit.

Coffee Punch

2 quarts strong coffee, cooled
1 cup whipping cream
1 cup milk
½ cup sugar
1½ teaspoons vanilla extract
1 quart vanilla ice cream
Garnish: grated chocolate

Combine coffee, whipping cream, milk, sugar, and vanilla; stir until sugar dissolves.

TO STORE: Refrigerate in a tightly covered container up to 2 days.

TO SERVE: Scoop ice cream into a punch bowl; gradually pour coffee mixture over ice cream. Ladle into cups, and garnish, if desired. Yield: about 1 gallon.

Blushing Orange Cooler

1 cup cranberry juice cocktail
1 (6-ounce) can frozen orange
    juice concentrate, thawed and
    undiluted
¼ cup sugar
2 cups club soda, chilled
Crushed ice
Garnishes: orange rind curls and
    fresh cranberries

Combine first 3 ingredients; stir until sugar dissolves.

TO STORE: Refrigerate in a tightly covered container up to 1 week.

TO SERVE: Add club soda to juice mixture. Serve over crushed ice. Garnish, if desired. Yield: about 4 cups.

Fruited Refrigerator Bran Muffins

1 cup diced mixed dried fruit
1½ cups all-purpose flour
2½ teaspoons baking powder
¼ teaspoon salt
1 cup shreds of wheat bran
    cereal
½ cup firmly packed brown
    sugar
¾ teaspoon pumpkin pie spice
1 egg, beaten
1 cup milk
¼ cup vegetable oil
1 teaspoon grated orange rind

Place fruit in a small bowl, and add boiling water to cover; let stand 5 minutes. Drain well; set aside.
Combine flour and next 5 ingredients in a medium bowl; make a well in center of mixture. Combine egg, milk, oil, and orange rind; add to dry ingredients, stirring just until moistened. Fold in fruit.

TO STORE: Refrigerate batter in a tightly covered container up to 1 week.

TO SERVE: Gently stir batter; spoon into greased muffin pans, filling three-fourths full. Bake at 400° for 15 to 20 minutes or until golden. Remove from pans immediately. Yield: 1 dozen.

Give your next brunch a special flair by welcoming guests with refreshing Blushing Orange Coolers and creamy Coffee Punch.

Refrigerator Buttermilk Pancakes

2 cups all-purpose flour
2½ teaspoons baking powder
1 teaspoon baking soda
¾ teaspoon salt
2 tablespoons sugar
2 eggs
2¼ cups buttermilk
¼ cup vegetable oil

Combine first 5 ingredients in a large bowl; stir well. Combine eggs, buttermilk, and oil; add to dry ingredients, stirring just until moistened.

TO STORE: Refrigerate batter in a tightly covered container up to 1 week.

TO SERVE: Gently stir batter. (If batter is too thick, gradually add milk or water to reach desired consistency.) For each pancake, pour about ¼ cup batter onto a hot, lightly greased griddle. Turn pancakes when tops are covered with bubbles and edges look cooked. Yield: 16 (4-inch) pancakes.

Blueberry Pancakes: Fold 1 cup fresh or frozen blueberries into batter just before cooking. Yield: 16 (4-inch) pancakes.

Overnight French Toast

8 (¾-inch-thick) slices French bread
4 eggs, beaten
1 cup milk
1 tablespoon sugar
½ teaspoon vanilla extract
¼ teaspoon ground cinnamon
2 tablespoons butter or margarine, divided
Honey-Orange Sauce

Place bread in a 13- x 9- x 2-inch baking dish. Combine eggs and next 4 ingredients; beat well. Pour egg mixture over bread; turn slices over to coat evenly.

TO STORE: Cover and refrigerate up to 8 hours.

TO SERVE: Melt 1 tablespoon butter in a large skillet over medium-high heat. Arrange 4 slices of bread in skillet; cook 3 minutes on each side or until browned. Remove to a serving plate, and keep warm. Repeat procedure with remaining 1 tablespoon butter and bread slices. Serve immediately with Honey-Orange Sauce. Yield: 4 servings.

Honey-Orange Sauce

1 cup unsweetened orange juice
2 tablespoons honey
2 teaspoons cornstarch
1 teaspoon grated orange rind
⅛ teaspoon ground ginger
1 (11-ounce) can mandarin oranges, drained

Combine first 5 ingredients in a saucepan. Cook over medium-high heat, stirring constantly, until mixture thickens. Remove from heat, and stir in oranges; cool.

TO STORE: Refrigerate in a tightly covered container up to 3 days.

TO SERVE: Microwave sauce at HIGH for 1½ to 2 minutes or until thoroughly heated, stirring once. Yield: 1½ cups.

You can linger over breakfast in bed when you serve Overnight French Toast with Honey-Orange Sauce.

Crunchy Granola Breakfast Bars

3½ cups regular oats, uncooked
½ cup flaked coconut
½ cup sliced almonds
½ cup wheat germ
¼ cup coarsely chopped
  cashews
¼ cup coarsely chopped pecans
¼ cup sesame seeds
¼ cup sunflower kernels
½ cup honey
¼ cup firmly packed brown
  sugar
¼ cup vegetable oil
½ cup creamy peanut butter
1 teaspoon vanilla extract

Combine first 8 ingredients in a large bowl; stir well, and set aside.

Combine honey, brown sugar, and oil in a small saucepan; cook over medium heat, stirring occasionally, until sugar dissolves and mixture is thoroughly heated. Remove from heat; add peanut butter and vanilla, stirring until peanut butter melts. Pour honey mixture over oats mixture; stir well. (Mixture will be dry at first; continue stirring until moist.)

Press mixture into a greased 15- x 10- x 1-inch jellyroll pan, using greased fingertips. Press mixture flat with the back of a wide metal spatula. Bake at 250° for 1 hour and 20 minutes or until golden brown. Cut into bars while warm; let cool completely in pan. Remove bars from pan.

TO STORE: Store in an airtight container at room temperature up to 1 week. Yield: 30 bars.

Turkey Sausage Muffin-wich

1 pound ground turkey
½ cup soft breadcrumbs
1 egg, lightly beaten
1 teaspoon ground sage
¾ teaspoon salt
¼ teaspoon crushed fennel
  seeds
¼ teaspoon dried red pepper
  flakes
⅛ teaspoon ground nutmeg
3 English muffins, split and
  toasted
6 (1-ounce) slices Cheddar
  cheese
Garnish: green pepper rings

Combine first 8 ingredients; mix well. Shape mixture into 6 patties.

TO STORE: Refrigerate patties in a tightly covered container up to 2 days. Freeze in a labeled airtight container up to 1 month.

TO SERVE: Cook patties in a large skillet over medium heat 10 to 15 minutes or until well browned. Drain on paper towels. Place 1 patty on each muffin half; top each with a slice of cheese. Broil about 6 inches from heat until cheese begins to melt. Garnish, if desired. Yield: 6 servings.

Kids of all ages will love Crunchy Granola Breakfast Bars. Packed in a lunchbox, they make a perfect mid-morning or afternoon snack.

Country Grits and Sausage Casserole

2 cups water
½ cup quick-cooking grits, uncooked
3½ cups (14 ounces) shredded extra-sharp Cheddar cheese
4 eggs, lightly beaten
1 cup milk
½ teaspoon dried whole thyme
⅛ teaspoon garlic powder
1½ pounds mild bulk pork sausage, cooked, crumbled, and drained
Garnishes: tomato wedges and fresh parsley sprigs

Bring water to a boil; stir in grits. Return to a boil; reduce heat to low, and cook 4 minutes, stirring occasionally. Add cheese, stirring until melted.

Combine eggs, milk, thyme, and garlic powder; stir well. Gradually stir about one-fourth of hot grits mixture into egg mixture; add to remaining hot mixture, stirring constantly. Stir in sausage. Pour into a lightly greased 11- x 7- x 1½-inch baking dish.

TO STORE: Cover and refrigerate up to 8 hours.

TO SERVE: Bake, uncovered, at 350° for 50 minutes or until set. Garnish, if desired. Yield: 6 to 8 servings.

Brunch Ham and Broccoli Bake

8 slices white bread, crust removed
1 cup diced cooked ham
1 cup frozen chopped broccoli, thawed and drained
3 eggs, lightly beaten
1½ cups milk
½ teaspoon dry mustard
¼ teaspoon onion salt
¼ teaspoon ground white pepper
2 cups (8 ounces) shredded Swiss cheese
Paprika

Place 4 slices of bread in a lightly greased 8-inch square baking dish. Sprinkle ham and broccoli over bread; top with remaining bread slices. Combine eggs and next 4 ingredients, stirring well; pour over bread. Sprinkle with cheese and paprika.

TO STORE: Cover and refrigerate up to 24 hours.

TO SERVE: Bake, uncovered, at 350° for 45 to 50 minutes or until puffed and golden brown. Serve immediately. Yield: 4 servings.

On cool autumn mornings, your family will enjoy waking up to the aroma of Country Grits and Sausage Casserole. Extra-sharp Cheddar cheese adds zip to this hearty dish.

Creamed Ham on Cornbread Cakes

½ cup chopped celery
½ cup chopped onion
¼ cup butter or margarine, melted
¼ cup all-purpose flour
¼ teaspoon salt
¼ teaspoon ground white pepper
2 cups milk
½ teaspoon Worcestershire sauce
2 cups diced cooked ham
½ cup diced cooked carrot
½ cup frozen English peas, thawed
1 tablespoon chopped fresh parsley
Cornbread Cakes
Garnish: fresh parsley sprigs

Sauté celery and onion in butter in a large skillet over medium heat until tender. Add flour, salt, and pepper, stirring until smooth. Cook 1 minute, stirring constantly. Gradually add milk and Worcestershire sauce; cook, stirring constantly, until mixture is thickened and bubbly. Stir in ham and next 3 ingredients. Cool slightly.

TO STORE: Refrigerate ham mixture in a tightly covered container up to 2 days. Freeze in a labeled airtight container up to 1 month.

TO SERVE: Cook over medium heat until hot, stirring often. Serve over Cornbread Cakes. Garnish, if desired. Yield: 4 to 6 servings.

Cornbread Cakes

1¾ cups self-rising cornmeal mix
1 egg, lightly beaten
1½ cups buttermilk
2 tablespoons butter or margarine, melted
¼ cup vegetable oil, divided

Combine first 4 ingredients in a large bowl, stirring just until moistened.

Heat 1 tablespoon oil in a large nonstick skillet over medium-high heat. Pour ⅓ cup batter into skillet for each corncake, cooking 3 cakes at a time. Cook 3 minutes on each side or until browned. Drain cakes on paper towels. Repeat procedure with remaining 3 tablespoons oil and batter. Cool completely.

TO STORE: Refrigerate cakes in a tightly covered container up to 2 days. Freeze in a labeled airtight container up to 1 month.

TO SERVE: Place cakes on ungreased baking sheets. Bake at 350° for 10 to 12 minutes or until thoroughly heated. Yield: 12 cakes.

Perfect for breakfast or brunch, individual servings of Creamed Ham on Cornbread Cakes are as attractive as they are delicious.

Brown·Bag Snacks

A great brown-bag lunch can rescue your day. The morning may have been frantic and the afternoon may not look much better, but a midday break for a homemade beef sandwich, hot soup, pasta salad, or cookies will restore your equilibrium.

This basic remedy for a stress-filled day involves some of the easiest cooking in this book. Children can help not only with the choices but also in the preparation of some of their favorites. They may not care to help make the sandwiches, but they will gladly help themselves to pitas stuffed with chicken or French rolls filled with vegetables when they're hungry and you're not around.

Then there is the diverse and delicious selection of spreads in this chapter. These can be turned into sandwiches or packed in small containers to be eaten with vegetable dippers or crackers. The main-course salads will travel well in zip-top plastic bags or, if there is no refrigerator at work, in chilled thermal containers. Freeze the soups in microwave-safe containers for quick reheating if a microwave oven is available. If you don't have access to a microwave oven, you may want to freeze the soups in vacuum-sealed bags so that you can heat them quickly in boiling water at home, and pour them into vacuum bottles.

Another way to enjoy brown-bag lunches—and dispense with the brown bag entirely—is to savor the food at home or on a picnic! You can look forward to easy sandwiches, salads, soups, and snacks ready to be taken no further than the table, TV room, or patio for Sunday suppers, late-night refreshments, brunches, or warm-weather meals.

For a deliciously complete lunch, be sure to include Chicken Pockets (page 51), Beefy Vegetable Soup (page 46), and Jumbo Cookies (page 57).

Creamy Chicken and Broccoli Soup

½ cup sliced fresh mushrooms
½ cup chopped onion
¼ cup butter or margarine,
  melted
¼ cup all-purpose flour
2 cups half-and-half
1½ cups chicken broth
1 cup diced cooked chicken
1 cup frozen chopped broccoli,
  thawed
½ teaspoon dried whole
  rosemary
½ teaspoon salt
¼ teaspoon dried whole thyme
¼ teaspoon pepper

Sauté mushrooms and onion in butter in a medium saucepan over low heat until tender; add flour, stirring until smooth. Cook 1 minute, stirring constantly. Gradually add half-and-half and chicken broth; cook over medium heat, stirring constantly, until mixture is thickened and bubbly. Stir in diced chicken and remaining ingredients. Cover and simmer 10 minutes, stirring occasionally. Cool.

TO STORE: Refrigerate soup in a tightly covered container up to 2 days. Freeze in a labeled airtight container up to 1 month.

TO SERVE: Cook over low heat until thoroughly heated, stirring occasionally. Yield: 4 cups.

Beefy Vegetable Soup

2 pounds ground beef
½ cup butter or margarine
½ cup all-purpose flour
1½ quarts water
1 cup chopped onion
1 (28-ounce) can tomatoes,
  undrained and chopped
1 (16-ounce) package frozen
  mixed vegetables
1 (15-ounce) can tomato sauce
  with tomato bits
1½ tablespoons beef-flavored
  bouillon granules
1½ teaspoons salt
2 teaspoons pepper

Cook ground beef in a large Dutch oven until meat is browned, stirring to crumble. Drain well, and set aside.

Melt butter in Dutch oven over low heat; add flour, stirring until smooth. Cook 1 minute, stirring constantly. Gradually add water; cook over medium heat, stirring constantly, until mixture is thickened and bubbly.

Add ground beef, onion, and remaining ingredients to mixture in Dutch oven. Bring to a boil; reduce heat, and simmer, uncovered, 1 hour. Cool.

TO STORE: Refrigerate soup in a tightly covered container up to 3 days. Freeze in a labeled airtight container up to 2 months.

TO SERVE: Cook over low heat until thoroughly heated, stirring occasionally. Yield: 13 cups.

Take a break from a busy day to enjoy the richness of Creamy Chicken and Broccoli Soup.

Versatile Pasta Salad

4 ounces rotini pasta, uncooked
1 cup sliced fresh mushrooms
1 cup broccoli flowerets
1 cup diced Cheddar cheese
½ cup shredded carrot
½ cup chopped sweet red
  pepper
¼ teaspoon seasoned salt
¼ teaspoon pepper
⅓ cup vegetable oil
¼ cup white wine vinegar
1 tablespoon Dijon mustard
¼ cup finely chopped green
  onions
1 tablespoon minced fresh
  parsley
2 cloves garlic, crushed
½ teaspoon sugar
½ teaspoon dried whole basil
¼ teaspoon salt
¼ teaspoon dried whole
  oregano
¼ teaspoon crushed red pepper
  flakes

Cook rotini according to package directions; drain. Rinse with cold water; drain again. Combine cooked pasta and next 7 ingredients in a large bowl. Set aside.

Combine vegetable oil and remaining ingredients in a jar. Cover tightly, and shake vigorously. Pour dressing over pasta mixture; toss well.

TO STORE: Refrigerate in a tightly covered container at least 2 hours and up to 3 days. Yield: 4½ cups.

Summer Pasta Salad: Substitute 1 small zucchini, thinly sliced, 1 small yellow squash, thinly sliced, and 6 to 8 cherry tomatoes, halved, for mushrooms and broccoli. Yield: about 4¾ cups.

Pasta Salad Roma: Substitute 1 (14-ounce) can artichoke hearts, drained and quartered, 1 cup cubed salami, 1 cup diced mozzarella cheese, and ½ cup sliced ripe olives for broccoli, carrot, and Cheddar cheese. Yield: 4 cups.

Tuna Tabbouleh

¾ cup bulgur wheat, uncooked
1 (12½-ounce) can
  water-packed tuna, drained
1 medium cucumber, peeled,
  seeded, and finely chopped
½ cup chopped onion
½ cup chopped fresh parsley
¼ cup pine nuts, toasted
¼ cup olive oil
¼ cup fresh lemon juice
1 tablespoon chopped fresh
  mint
1 clove garlic, crushed
1 teaspoon grated lemon rind
½ teaspoon salt
¼ teaspoon pepper
8 to 10 cherry tomatoes, halved

Place bulgur in a colander; rinse with cold water, and drain well. Combine bulgur, tuna, cucumber, onion, parsley, and pine nuts; stir well. Set aside.

Combine oil and next 6 ingredients in a jar. Cover tightly, and shake vigorously. Pour dressing over bulgur mixture; toss well.

TO STORE: Refrigerate in a tightly covered container at least 2 hours and up to 2 days.

TO SERVE: Stir in tomato halves. Yield: 6½ cups.

Tortellini-Vegetable Salad

1 (9-ounce) package fresh
   cheese-filled tortellini
½ cup broccoli flowerets
½ cup cauliflower flowerets
6 to 8 cherry tomatoes, halved
½ small sweet red pepper, cut
   into ¼-inch strips
½ small green pepper, cut into
   ¼-inch strips
½ small purple onion, thinly
   sliced
½ cup commercial Italian salad
   dressing

Cook tortellini according to package directions; drain. Combine cooked tortellini and next 6 ingredients in a large bowl. Pour dressing over pasta mixture; toss well.

TO STORE: Refrigerate in a tightly covered container at least 2 hours and up to 3 days. Yield: 5 cups.

Chunky Peanut Butter Spread

2 cups chunky peanut butter
⅓ cup finely chopped dates
⅓ cup finely chopped dried
   apple
3 tablespoons honey
1 tablespoon orange juice
2 teaspoons grated orange rind

Combine all ingredients; stir well.

TO STORE: Refrigerate in a tightly covered container up to 1 week.

TO SERVE: Serve with crackers, or use as a spread for sandwiches, split bagels, or toast. Yield: 2⅔ cups.

Pimiento Cheese Spread

1 (8-ounce) package cream
   cheese, softened
1 cup (4 ounces) shredded
   sharp Cheddar cheese
1 cup (4 ounces) shredded
   American cheese
½ cup mayonnaise
2 (4-ounce) jars diced pimiento,
   drained
2 teaspoons Worcestershire
   sauce
1 teaspoon dry mustard
¼ teaspoon garlic powder
⅛ teaspoon hot sauce

Beat cream cheese at medium speed of an electric mixer. Stir in Cheddar cheese and remaining ingredients.

TO STORE: Refrigerate in a tightly covered container up to 2 weeks.

TO SERVE: Serve with crackers, or use as a spread for sandwiches. Yield: 3 cups.

Nutty Carrot-Cheese Spread

1 (8-ounce) package cream
　cheese, softened
1 cup shredded carrot
¾ cup (3 ounces) shredded
　Cheddar cheese
½ cup chopped pecans, toasted
¼ cup currants
¼ cup plus 2 tablespoons
　orange juice

Combine all ingredients, stirring well.

TO STORE: Refrigerate in a tightly covered container up to 1 week.

TO SERVE: Serve with crackers, or use as a spread for sandwiches. Yield: 2 cups.

Chock-full of carrots, pecans, and currants, Nutty Carrot-Cheese Spread is a treat in sandwiches or on your favorite crackers.

Savory Ham and Cheese Spread

1 (8-ounce) package cream
  cheese, softened
1 cup ground cooked ham
¼ cup grated Parmesan cheese
¼ cup finely chopped onion
2 tablespoons mayonnaise
1 tablespoon chopped fresh
  parsley
1 teaspoon dried Italian
  seasoning

Combine all ingredients, stirring well.

TO STORE: Refrigerate in a tightly covered container up to 1 week.

TO SERVE: Serve with crackers, or use as a spread for sandwiches. Yield: 2 cups.

Chicken Pockets

3 cups finely chopped cooked
  chicken
⅔ cup mayonnaise or salad
  dressing
½ cup thinly sliced celery
½ cup chopped cashews
¼ cup raisins
¼ cup finely chopped dried
  apricots
2 tablespoons chopped onion
½ teaspoon salt
¼ teaspoon ground white
  pepper
4 (6-inch) whole wheat pita
  bread rounds, cut in half
Shredded lettuce

Combine first 9 ingredients; stir well. Spoon mixture evenly into pita bread halves.

TO STORE: Refrigerate sandwiches in a tightly covered container up to 2 days. Freeze in a labeled airtight container up to 2 weeks.

TO SERVE: Thaw before serving. Top with shredded lettuce. Yield: 8 servings.

Baked Ham and Swiss Sandwiches

½ cup butter or margarine,
  softened
2 tablespoons minced onion
1 tablespoon poppy seeds
1 tablespoon Dijon mustard
½ teaspoon Worcestershire
  sauce
8 hamburger buns, split
16 (1-ounce) slices cooked ham
8 (1-ounce) slices Swiss cheese

Combine first 5 ingredients, stirring well. Spread butter mixture evenly on cut sides of hamburger buns. For each sandwich, place 2 slices of ham and 1 slice of cheese on bottom half of each bun; cover with top half of bun. Wrap each sandwich in aluminum foil.

TO STORE: Refrigerate up to 3 days.

TO SERVE: Place aluminum foil-wrapped sandwiches on a baking sheet. Bake at 350° for 20 to 25 minutes or until sandwiches are thoroughly heated and cheese is melted. Yield: 8 servings.

Sandwich Boats Español

1 (15-ounce) can black beans,
  drained and rinsed
1 (11-ounce) can whole kernel
  corn with red and green
  peppers, drained
1 small tomato, seeded and
  chopped
½ cup (2 ounces) shredded
  sharp Cheddar cheese
½ cup (2 ounces) shredded
  Monterey Jack cheese with
  jalapeño peppers
3 tablespoons chopped purple
  onion
3 tablespoons mayonnaise or
  salad dressing
2 tablespoons catsup
¼ teaspoon salt
¼ teaspoon dried whole
  oregano
¼ teaspoon pepper
⅛ teaspoon garlic powder
8 (6-inch) French rolls
Curly leaf lettuce

Combine first 6 ingredients in a medium bowl. Combine mayonnaise, catsup, salt, oregano, pepper, and garlic powder in a small bowl, stirring well. Add mayonnaise mixture to bean mixture, stirring to coat thoroughly.

TO STORE: Refrigerate bean mixture in a tightly covered container up to 3 days.

TO SERVE: Cut a ½-inch-thick slice from top of each roll. Carefully remove soft bread from inside bottom part of each roll, leaving about ¼-inch-thick shells. (Reserve soft bread for other uses.) Line rolls with lettuce leaves, and fill evenly with bean mixture; replace tops. Yield: 8 servings.

Beef Sandwiches with Onion Marmalade

1 cup coarsely chopped onion
1 cup coarsely chopped purple
  onion
3 green onions, chopped
2 tablespoons vegetable oil
¼ cup sugar
2 tablespoons cider vinegar
1 teaspoon Worcestershire sauce
¼ teaspoon salt
⅛ teaspoon pepper
Dash of ground cloves
Curly endive leaves
4 (6-inch) French rolls, split
  lengthwise and toasted
¾ pound thinly sliced roast beef

Sauté onions in oil in a large saucepan over medium-low heat 1 hour or until very tender, stirring occasionally. Stir in sugar and next 5 ingredients. Cook over low heat, stirring occasionally, 25 to 30 minutes or until liquid evaporates. Cool completely.

TO STORE: Refrigerate in a tightly covered container up to 1 week.

TO SERVE: Bring onion mixture to room temperature. Place endive on bottom halves of toasted rolls; arrange beef over endive. Spread onion mixture evenly over beef; place top halves on rolls. Cut each sandwich in half. Yield: 4 servings.

Add a new and exciting flavor to brown-bag lunches. Beef Sandwiches with Onion Marmalade will satisfy the heartiest appetite.

Pepperoni-Vegetable Rolls

1 (8-ounce) package cream
  cheese, softened
1 (3½-ounce) package sliced
  pepperoni, chopped
½ cup chopped onion
½ cup chopped celery
½ cup chopped green pepper
1 clove garlic, minced
1 tablespoon tomato paste
¼ teaspoon dried Italian
  seasoning
⅛ teaspoon pepper
6 (3½-inch) French rolls

Combine first 9 ingredients in a small bowl; stir well, and set aside.

Cut a ½-inch-thick slice from top of each roll. Carefully remove soft bread from inside bottom part of each roll, leaving about ¼-inch-thick shells. (Reserve soft bread for other uses.)

Fill bottom part of each roll with ⅓ cup cream cheese mixture; replace tops.

TO STORE: Refrigerate sandwiches in a tightly covered container up to 2 days. Freeze sandwiches in a labeled airtight container up to 2 weeks.

TO SERVE: Thaw before serving. Yield: 6 servings.

Tropical Nut Bread Sandwiches

½ cup chopped dates
½ cup chopped pecans or
  walnuts
½ teaspoon baking soda
½ cup hot water
2 tablespoons shortening
⅓ cup sugar
1 egg
1 cup all-purpose flour
¼ teaspoon salt
½ teaspoon vanilla extract
Pineapple-Cheese Spread

Combine dates, pecans, and soda in a small bowl. Stir in hot water; set aside to cool.

Cream shortening in a medium bowl; gradually add sugar, beating well at medium speed of an electric mixer. Add egg, and beat well.

Combine flour and salt; add to creamed mixture alternately with date mixture, beginning and ending with flour mixture. Mix just until blended after each addition. Stir in vanilla.

Pour batter into 2 greased and floured 16-ounce vegetable cans. Bake at 350° for 35 to 40 minutes or until a wooden pick inserted in center comes out clean. Cool in cans 10 minutes; remove loaves from cans, and cool on wire racks. Slice loaves into ¼-inch-thick slices. Spread Pineapple-Cheese Spread evenly over half the bread slices. Top with remaining bread slices.

TO STORE: Refrigerate sandwiches in a tightly covered container up to 2 days. Freeze sandwiches in a labeled airtight container up to 2 weeks.

TO SERVE: Thaw before serving. Yield: 8 servings.

Pineapple-Cheese Spread

2 (3-ounce) packages cream
  cheese, softened
⅓ cup crushed pineapple,
  drained
¼ cup flaked coconut
2 tablespoons pineapple
  preserves

Combine all ingredients in a small bowl; stir well. Yield: 1¼ cups.

Tropical Nut Bread Sandwiches with Pineapple-Cheese Spread are a tasty snack to enjoy on the patio or by the pool.

Turkey and Cheese Rolls

1 (0.7-ounce) envelope Italian
  salad dressing mix
¼ cup Dijon mustard
2 teaspoons sugar
8 (1-ounce) slices Swiss or
  Provolone cheese
8 (2-ounce) slices cooked turkey
  breast
1 cup alfalfa sprouts

Combine first 3 ingredients; set aside.

Place 1 cheese slice on top of each turkey slice; spread evenly with mustard mixture. Top each with 2 table-spoons alfalfa sprouts, and roll up jellyroll fashion, starting at short end. Secure each roll with a wooden pick.

TO STORE: Refrigerate in a tightly covered container up to 3 days. Yield: 8 servings.

Jumbo Cookies

2 cups creamy peanut butter
½ cup butter or margarine,
  softened
1 cup sugar
1 cup plus 2 tablespoons firmly
  packed brown sugar
3 eggs
¾ teaspoon light corn syrup
¼ teaspoon vanilla extract
4½ cups regular oats, uncooked
2 teaspoons baking soda
¼ teaspoon salt
1 cup candy-coated chocolate
  pieces
1 (6-ounce) package semisweet
  chocolate morsels

Cream peanut butter and butter; gradually add sugars, beating well at medium speed of an electric mixer. Add eggs, corn syrup, and vanilla, beating well. Combine oats, soda, and salt; add to creamed mixture, mixing well. Stir in chocolate pieces and morsels. (Dough will be stiff.)

For each cookie, pack dough into a ¼-cup measure. Drop dough, 4 inches apart, onto lightly greased cookie sheets. Lightly press each cookie into a 3½-inch circle. Bake at 350° for 10 to 12 minutes or until lightly browned. Cool slightly on cookie sheets; remove cookies to wire racks to cool completely.

TO STORE: Store cookies in an airtight container at room temperature up to 1 week. Freeze in a labeled airtight container up to 1 month.

TO SERVE: Thaw cookies at room temperature. Yield: 2½ dozen.

No-Bake Chocolate Oatmeal Cookies

2 cups sugar
¼ cup cocoa
½ cup milk
¼ cup butter or margarine
2½ cups regular oats, uncooked
¾ cup creamy peanut butter
2 teaspoons vanilla extract

Combine first 4 ingredients in a heavy saucepan. Cook over medium heat, stirring occasionally, until mixture comes to a boil; boil 1 minute. Remove from heat; add oats, peanut butter, and vanilla, stirring well. Drop dough by heaping teaspoonfuls onto lightly greased wax paper. Cool completely.

TO STORE: Store in an airtight container at room temperature up to 2 weeks. Yield: 4½ dozen.

Pack Turkey and Cheese Rolls in the ice chest to take along and enjoy at your next summer outing.

Double·Duty

Make something special this weekend—maybe a big golden turkey with cornbread stuffing or a beautiful ham glazed with cranberry sauce. The recipes in this chapter show you how the leftovers of large cuts of meat and large batches of spaghetti sauce, rice, and beans are a make-ahead dividend, an already cooked ingredient for other quick meals to come.

For example, what starts out as Sunday's pot roast can become Wednesday's stroganoff. Baked ham becomes a tangy ham loaf; roast chicken turns elegant in a warm salad with walnuts and grapes.

If you can't warm up to the thought of leftovers, you may decide to freeze the surplus and retrieve it several weeks later. It will be easier to use if you divide the meat into convenient cooking quantities, measured in pounds or cups, and label the container. Sliced or diced meats will stay fresh-tasting longer if you moisten them with some of the pan juices before freezing.

In the summer, when you don't want to heat up the kitchen, it makes sense to grill extra portions of pork, beef, or poultry. Then turn the extras into cool salads and sandwiches to be eaten later.

The latter part of this chapter is devoted to beans and rice. You will find that it's well worth cooking extra amounts of these two basics to have them left over for Home-Style Baked Beans, Hearty Sausage-Bean Soup, Pork Fried Rice, and Rice Pudding.

Meaty Spaghetti Sauce (page 70) can be made ahead and frozen. Later, it can be made into Stuffed Shells Florentine (page 71).

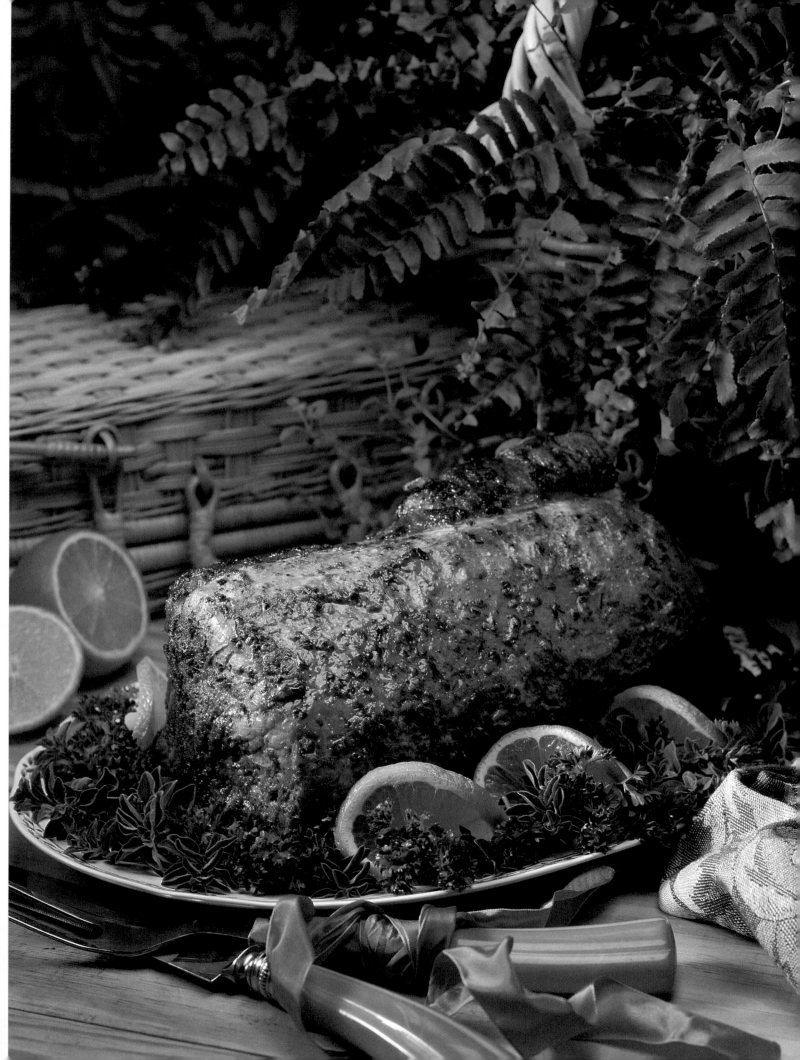

Roast Loin of Pork

1 (5- to 6-pound) pork loin
   roast
4 cloves garlic, minced
1 tablespoon dried whole
   oregano
2 teaspoons ground cumin
½ teaspoon pepper
½ cup orange juice

Trim fat from roast. Place roast on a rack in a roasting pan. Combine garlic and next 3 ingredients; rub garlic mixture over roast. Pour orange juice over roast.

Insert meat thermometer in roast, making sure it does not touch fat or bone. Cover and bake at 325° for 2½ hours. Uncover and bake 30 minutes or until meat thermometer registers 160° (medium). Let roast stand 10 to 15 minutes before serving.

TO STORE: Remove remaining meat from bone. Slice or chop meat as desired. Refrigerate meat in a tightly covered container up to 4 days. Freeze in a labeled airtight container up to 3 months. Yield: 12 to 14 servings.

Sesame Noodles with Roast Pork

6 ounces vermicelli or thin
   spaghetti, uncooked
¼ cup plus 1 tablespoon rice
   wine vinegar
2 tablespoons dark sesame oil,
   divided
1 tablespoon vegetable oil
2 teaspoons hoisin sauce
1 teaspoon soy sauce
1 tablespoon minced fresh
   gingerroot
1 clove garlic, minced
¾ pound cooked pork roast, cut
   into thin strips
½ pound fresh spinach
3 tablespoons sesame seeds,
   toasted
Salt and pepper to taste

Cook pasta according to package directions; drain. Place pasta in a large bowl.

Combine vinegar, 1 tablespoon sesame oil, vegetable oil, hoisin sauce, soy sauce, gingerroot, and garlic in a small bowl; stir well. Pour half of dressing over pasta, tossing to combine.

Heat remaining 1 tablespoon sesame oil in a large skillet over medium-high heat. Add pork; sauté 3 to 5 minutes or until browned. Add pork to pasta mixture, tossing gently to combine.

Remove stems from spinach; wash leaves thoroughly. Cut spinach into thin strips. Cook in a large nonstick skillet over medium-high heat 3 to 4 minutes or just until spinach wilts. Add spinach to noodle mixture. Sprinkle with sesame seeds, and pour remaining dressing over pasta; toss gently to combine. Add salt and pepper to taste. Serve warm. Yield: 4 servings.

Garnished with orange twists and fresh parsley and sage sprigs, Roast Loin of Pork is an elegant entrée.

Warm Roast Pork-Potato Salad

1 (13¾-ounce) can chicken
  broth, undiluted
1½ pounds new potatoes,
  quartered
1 medium-size purple onion,
  quartered and thinly sliced
1 cup frozen English peas,
  thawed
½ cup sliced ripe olives
½ cup chopped fresh parsley
Pepper to taste
⅓ cup olive oil or vegetable oil
2½ tablespoons cider vinegar
¼ teaspoon ground cumin
⅛ teaspoon chili powder
¾ pound cubed cooked pork
  roast
2 tablespoons dry vermouth
2 hard-cooked eggs, coarsely
  chopped

Bring chicken broth to a boil in a medium saucepan. Add potato; cover, reduce heat, and simmer 10 to 15 minutes or until potato is tender. Remove potato from broth, reserving broth. Place potato in a large bowl; add onion and next 4 ingredients, tossing gently to combine.

Cook reserved broth over medium heat until reduced to ½ cup. Pour over potato mixture; toss gently to combine.

Combine oil, vinegar, cumin, and chili powder in a medium saucepan; stir well. Add pork and vermouth. Cook over medium heat until thoroughly heated. Add pork mixture to potato mixture, tossing gently. Add eggs, tossing gently to combine. Serve warm. Yield: 6 servings.

Black Beans and Pork over Rice

1 teaspoon ground cumin
½ teaspoon ground coriander
¼ teaspoon chili powder
½ pound diced cooked pork
  roast
⅓ cup orange juice
1 medium onion, chopped
1¼ cups chopped sweet red
  pepper
2 cloves garlic, minced
2 tablespoons vegetable oil
1 (16-ounce) can black beans,
  drained and rinsed
1 medium tomato, seeded and
  chopped
2 tablespoons chopped green
  chiles
¼ teaspoon salt
⅛ teaspoon pepper
3 cups hot cooked rice
Garnish: fresh cilantro sprigs

Combine cumin, coriander, and chili powder; toss pork in spice mixture to coat. Heat a large skillet over medium-high heat until hot; add pork. Cook, stirring constantly, 2 minutes or until thoroughly heated. Remove pork from skillet, and place in a medium bowl; add orange juice, stirring well. Set aside.

Sauté onion, sweet pepper, and garlic in oil in skillet until vegetables are tender. Stir in reserved pork mixture, beans, and next 4 ingredients. Cook, stirring occasionally, until thoroughly heated. Serve over rice. Garnish, if desired. Yield: 4 servings.

Green chiles, cumin, and garlic give Black Beans and Pork over Rice an authentic south-of-the-border flavor.

Roast Pork Sandwiches

½ cup mayonnaise
1 tablespoon orange juice
1 teaspoon grated orange rind
Dash of hot sauce
1 (16-ounce) loaf Italian bread,
 sliced in half lengthwise
1 pound thinly sliced cooked
 pork roast
1 medium tomato, thinly sliced
1 small purple onion, thinly
 sliced and separated into rings
Salt and pepper to taste

Combine first 4 ingredients; stir well. Spread cut sides of bread with mayonnaise mixture. Layer pork, tomato, and onion on bottom slice of bread; sprinkle with salt and pepper. Cover with top slice of bread. Cut sandwich into fourths. Yield: 4 servings.

Cranberry-Glazed Ham

1 (12- to 14-pound) smoked,
  fully cooked ham
2 tablespoons Dijon mustard
Whole cloves
1 (16-ounce) can jellied
  cranberry sauce
2 tablespoons red wine vinegar
1 tablespoon soy sauce
1 tablespoon minced fresh
  gingerroot
1 teaspoon dry mustard
¼ teaspoon ground cardamom
¼ teaspoon ground cinnamon
⅛ teaspoon ground nutmeg
Garnishes: flowering cabbage
  and fresh cranberries
1½ cups ruby port wine
¾ cup sugar
1 (12-ounce) package fresh
  cranberries

Trim skin from ham, leaving ¼-inch thickness of fat. Brush ham with Dijon mustard. Score fat on ham in a diamond design, and stud with cloves. Place ham, fat side up, on a rack in a shallow roasting pan. Insert meat thermometer, making sure it does not touch fat or bone. Bake, uncovered, at 250° for 2 hours.

Place cranberry sauce in a medium saucepan; add vinegar and soy sauce. Cook over low heat, stirring frequently, until cranberry sauce melts. Stir in gingerroot and next 4 ingredients. Spread one-third of cranberry sauce mixture over ham. Cover and bake at 350° for 1 hour or until thermometer registers 140° (18 to 24 minutes per pound), basting with cranberry sauce mixture after 30 minutes. Let stand 20 minutes before slicing. Garnish, if desired.

Add wine and sugar to remaining cranberry sauce mixture; bring to a boil. Stir in cranberries, and cook over medium heat 15 minutes or until cranberries pop. Remove from heat; let stand 20 minutes. Serve with ham.

TO STORE: Remove remaining meat from bone. Slice or chop meat as desired. Refrigerate in a tightly covered container up to 1 week. Freeze in a labeled airtight container up to 3 months. (Ham bone may be frozen in a labeled airtight container up to 6 months for later use.) Yield: 20 to 25 servings.

Ham and Bean Soup

1 pound dried Great Northern
  beans
6 cups water, divided
1 medium onion, chopped
2 cloves garlic, crushed
1 medium-size hot red pepper
1 bay leaf
2 teaspoons salt
½ teaspoon dried whole thyme
¼ teaspoon pepper
4 medium potatoes, peeled and
  cubed
3 medium carrots, scraped and
  cut into ½-inch slices
2 cups coarsely chopped cooked
  ham

Sort and wash beans; place in a Dutch oven. Cover with water 2 inches above beans; let soak 8 hours.

Drain beans and return to Dutch oven. Add 4 cups water and next 7 ingredients. Bring to a boil; cover, reduce heat, and simmer 1½ hours, stirring occasionally. Add remaining 2 cups water, potato, carrot, and ham. Cover and simmer 30 minutes, or until vegetables are tender. Remove hot red pepper and bay leaf before serving. Yield: 10 cups.

Cranberry-Glazed Ham is a welcome addition to any holiday meal. String fresh cranberries for a garnish with extra flair.

Scalloped Ham and Potatoes

¼ cup butter or margarine
¼ cup all-purpose flour
2 cups half-and-half
¾ teaspoon salt
¼ teaspoon ground white
  pepper
4 medium potatoes, peeled and
  thinly sliced
2 cups chopped cooked ham
2 small onions, thinly sliced and
  separated into rings
¼ cup chopped green pepper
2 cloves garlic, minced

Melt butter in a heavy saucepan over low heat; add flour, stirring until smooth. Cook 1 minute, stirring constantly. Gradually add half-and-half; cook over medium heat, stirring constantly, until mixture is thickened and bubbly. Stir in salt and white pepper.

Spoon ¼ cup sauce mixture into a greased 10-inch ovenproof skillet. Combine potato and remaining ingredients in a large bowl; stir well. Layer half of potato mixture over sauce. Top with half of remaining sauce. Repeat layers. Cover and bake at 350° for 1 hour or until potato is tender. Yield: 8 servings.

Crustless Ham Quiche

1 cup diced cooked ham
½ pound fresh mushrooms,
  sliced
1 tablespoon butter or
  margarine, melted
4 eggs
1 cup sour cream
1 cup small-curd cottage cheese
½ cup grated Parmesan cheese
¼ cup all-purpose flour
½ teaspoon dried whole
  dillweed
½ teaspoon dry mustard
⅛ teaspoon ground nutmeg
⅛ teaspoon pepper
1 cup (4 ounces) shredded
  Swiss cheese
½ cup chopped fresh parsley

Cook ham in a skillet over medium heat until lightly browned; set aside. Sauté mushrooms in butter in a skillet over medium heat until tender (about 10 minutes). Sprinkle mushrooms and reserved ham evenly in a greased 10-inch quiche dish.

Combine eggs and next 8 ingredients in container of an electric blender; process until smooth. Stir cheese and parsley into egg mixture; pour over ham and mushrooms. Bake at 350° for 40 to 45 minutes or until set. Let stand 10 minutes before serving. Yield: one 10-inch quiche.

Put leftover ham to use in Crustless Ham Quiche. This hearty meat and egg pie is a tasty, no-fuss dish.

Sweet-Sour Ham Loaf

1 pound ground cooked ham
1 pound ground pork
2 eggs, lightly beaten
¾ cup soft breadcrumbs
½ cup milk
¼ cup plus 1 tablespoon
  Chinese sweet-and-sour sauce,
  divided
2 tablespoons brown sugar
2 tablespoons soy sauce, divided
1 tablespoon plus 1 teaspoon
  Dijon mustard, divided

Combine first 5 ingredients, mixing well. Add 3 tablespoons sweet-and-sour sauce, brown sugar, 2 teaspoons soy sauce, and 2 teaspoons mustard; mix well. Press mixture into a greased 9- x 5- x 3-inch loafpan.

Combine remaining 2 tablespoons sweet-and-sour sauce, 1 tablespoon plus 1 teaspoon soy sauce, and 2 teaspoons mustard in a small bowl; stir well. Pour sauce over ham loaf. Bake at 350° for 1 hour and 15 minutes. Yield: 6 to 8 servings.

Savory Roast Chickens

2 (3½- to 4-pound)
   broiler-fryers
½ teaspoon salt
½ teaspoon garlic powder
2 carrots, scraped and sliced
2 stalks celery with leaves,
   sliced
1 large onion, cut into wedges
10 fresh parsley sprigs
2 teaspoons dried whole
   rosemary
2 teaspoons dried whole
   tarragon
¼ cup butter or margarine,
   melted
1 cup chicken broth

Remove giblets and necks from chickens; reserve for other uses. Rinse chickens thoroughly inside and out with cold water; pat dry. Sprinkle body cavities of chickens with salt and garlic powder; set aside.

Combine carrot and next 5 ingredients in a medium bowl. Lightly pack the vegetable mixture into body cavities of chickens. Close cavities with skewers and truss. Tie ends of legs together with string. Lift wingtips up and over back, and tuck under chickens.

Place chickens, breast side up, on a rack in a roasting pan. Brush chickens with butter. Pour chicken broth over chickens.

Insert meat thermometer in breast or meaty part of thigh, making sure it does not touch bone. Cover and bake at 325° for 1½ hours, basting frequently with chicken broth. Uncover and bake an additional 1½ hours or until meat thermometer registers 185°, basting frequently with chicken broth. If chicken starts to brown too much, cover with aluminum foil. Let stand 10 minutes before serving. Yield: 8 to 10 servings.

TO STORE: Remove remaining meat from bone. Slice or chop meat as desired. Refrigerate in a tightly covered container up to 3 days. Freeze in a labeled airtight container up to 3 months.

Warm Chinese Chicken Salad

¼ cup cider vinegar
2 tablespoons walnut oil
2 tablespoons vegetable oil
2 tablespoons chicken broth
1 teaspoon dried whole tarragon
½ teaspoon Dijon mustard
½ teaspoon Worcestershire
   sauce
¼ teaspoon salt
⅛ teaspoon ground nutmeg
2 cups torn Chinese cabbage
2 cups torn romaine lettuce
⅔ cup chopped walnuts, toasted
3 cups coarsely chopped cooked
   chicken
1½ cups halved seedless red
   grapes

Combine first 9 ingredients in a small bowl, stirring well. Toss cabbage and lettuce with half of dressing mixture in a large shallow bowl. Sprinkle walnuts over cabbage mixture.

Combine chicken and 3 tablespoons remaining dressing mixture in a skillet over medium heat. Cook, stirring occasionally, until chicken is thoroughly heated. Toss hot chicken mixture and grape halves with cabbage mixture. Serve salad warm with remaining dressing. Yield: 4 servings.

A tangy dressing gives cooked chicken an Oriental flavor in elegant Warm Chinese Chicken Salad.

Chicken Flautas with Avocado Sauce

1 ripe avocado, peeled and
  mashed
½ cup finely chopped fresh
  cilantro
¼ cup sour cream
2 tablespoons fresh lime juice
1 green onion, thinly sliced
¼ teaspoon salt
¼ teaspoon pepper
1 small onion, minced
2 cloves garlic, minced
½ cup chicken broth
2 cups shredded cooked chicken
¼ cup drained chopped green
  chiles
¼ teaspoon salt
¼ teaspoon chili powder
10 (6-inch) corn tortillas
Vegetable oil
Garnish: chopped fresh tomato

Combine first 7 ingredients, stirring well; set avocado sauce aside.

Place onion, garlic, and broth in a medium skillet; cover and cook over medium-low heat 15 minutes. Stir in chicken, chiles, ¼ teaspoon salt, and chili powder; cook over medium heat until thoroughly heated.

Place 3 tablespoons chicken mixture in center of each tortilla; roll up tortillas, and secure with wooden picks.

Fry tortilla rolls in hot oil (375°) in a large skillet until golden brown on all sides. Drain on paper towels. Serve with reserved avocado sauce. Garnish, if desired. Yield: 4 servings.

Chicken Fettuccine

½ pound fresh mushrooms,
  sliced
1 small sweet red pepper, cut
  into thin strips
1 small onion, chopped
1 clove garlic, crushed
2 tablespoons butter or
  margarine, melted
3 cups chopped cooked chicken
1 (8-ounce) package fettuccine
½ cup whipping cream
½ cup butter or margarine
½ cup grated Parmesan cheese
2 tablespoons chopped fresh
  parsley
¼ teaspoon ground white
  pepper

Sauté first 4 ingredients in 2 tablespoons butter in a large skillet over medium heat until vegetables are tender. Add chicken, and cook until thoroughly heated. Set aside, and keep warm.

Cook fettuccine according to package directions; drain and place in a large bowl.

Combine whipping cream and ½ cup butter in a small saucepan; cook over low heat until butter melts. Stir in Parmesan cheese, chopped parsley, and white pepper. Pour whipping cream mixture over hot fettuccine; add chicken mixture. Toss until fettuccine is thoroughly coated. Yield: 6 to 8 servings.

Chicken Fettuccine is impressive, yet easy to make. Add bread and a favorite beverage for a complete meal.

Toasted Chicken and Swiss Sandwiches

3 tablespoons mayonnaise
1½ tablespoons coarse-grained mustard
8 slices rye or pumpernickel bread
½ pound thinly sliced cooked chicken
4 slices bacon, cooked
4 (1-ounce) slices Swiss cheese
2 eggs, lightly beaten
3 tablespoons milk
1 to 4 tablespoons butter or margarine

Combine mayonnaise and mustard, stirring well. Spread mayonnaise mixture on one side of each slice of bread. Arrange chicken on 4 slices of bread; top with bacon, cheese, and remaining bread slices.

Combine eggs and milk, stirring well. Melt 1 tablespoon butter in a large skillet over medium heat. Carefully dip one sandwich into egg mixture, coating both sides. Cook in melted butter until golden brown and cheese is slightly melted, turning once. Repeat procedure with remaining sandwiches, adding 1 tablespoon butter to skillet each time, if necessary. Yield: 4 servings.

Roast Turkey with Cornbread Stuffing

2 medium onions, chopped
1¼ cups chopped celery
2 large cloves garlic, minced
3 tablespoons butter or margarine, melted
4 slices white bread
4 cups crumbled cornbread
1 cup finely chopped fresh parsley
1 teaspoon rubbed sage
1 teaspoon dried whole rosemary
½ teaspoon salt
½ teaspoon dried whole thyme
⅛ teaspoon ground nutmeg
⅛ teaspoon pepper
2 cups chicken broth, divided
3 eggs, lightly beaten
1 (14- to 16-pound) turkey
Melted butter or margarine or vegetable oil
Garnishes: fresh parsley sprigs, fresh thyme sprigs, fresh sage sprigs, and crab apples

Sauté onion, celery, and garlic in 3 tablespoons butter in a large skillet over medium heat until tender. Set aside. Trim crust from bread slices; reserve crust for other uses. Cut bread into cubes. Combine bread, cornbread, and next 7 ingredients in a large bowl. Add onion mixture, 1 cup chicken broth, and eggs; stir until bread mixture is moistened.

Remove giblets and neck from turkey; reserve for other uses, if desired. Rinse turkey thoroughly with cold water; pat dry. Lightly pack stuffing into body cavities of turkey. Tuck legs under flap of skin around tail, or close cavity with skewers and truss. Tie ends of tail with cord. Lift wingtips up and over back, and tuck under turkey.

Place turkey on a rack in a roasting pan, breast side up; brush entire turkey with butter. Insert meat thermometer in meaty part of thigh, making sure it does not touch bone. Pour remaining 1 cup broth in bottom of pan. Cover turkey with heavy-duty aluminum foil, and bake at 325° for 3 hours. Uncover and bake an additional 2 to 2½ hours or until thermometer reaches 185°, basting every 30 minutes with butter.

When turkey is two-thirds done, cut the cord or band of skin holding the drumstick ends to the tail; this will ensure that the thighs are cooked internally. Turkey is done when drumsticks are easy to move up and down. Let stand 15 minutes before carving. Garnish, if desired.

TO STORE: Remove remaining meat from bones. Slice or chop meat as desired. Refrigerate in a tightly covered container up to 3 days. Freeze in a labeled airtight container up to 3 months. (Turkey carcass may be frozen in a labeled airtight container up to 6 months for later use.) Yield: 24 to 26 servings.

Day-After-Thanksgiving Sandwiches

4 ounces cream cheese, softened
½ cup jellied cranberry sauce
8 slices white bread or whole wheat bread
Curly leaf lettuce
¾ pound sliced cooked turkey
Salt and pepper to taste

Beat cream cheese at medium speed of an electric mixer until smooth. Spread cream cheese and cranberry sauce evenly over one side of 4 slices of bread. Top each slice with lettuce; divide turkey evenly over lettuce. Sprinkle with salt and pepper; top with remaining bread slices. Yield: 4 servings.

Make tender Roast Turkey with Cornbread Stuffing the centerpiece of your holiday table.

Curried Turkey Salad

3 cups chopped cooked turkey
2 stalks celery, sliced
½ cup frozen English peas, thawed
½ cup finely chopped fresh parsley
⅓ cup mayonnaise
2 tablespoons sour cream
2 teaspoons fresh lime juice or lemon juice
1½ teaspoons curry powder
½ teaspoon ground cumin
¼ teaspoon salt
¼ teaspoon pepper
⅛ teaspoon ground cinnamon
⅛ teaspoon ground nutmeg
½ cup sliced almonds, toasted
Lettuce leaves

Combine turkey, celery, peas, and parsley in a medium bowl; stir well. Combine mayonnaise and next 8 ingredients in a small bowl; pour over turkey mixture, tossing well. Chill thoroughly.

Before serving, add almonds to salad, and toss well. Serve on lettuce leaves. Yield: 4 servings.

Turkey Vegetable Soup

1 turkey carcass
3 quarts water
1 bay leaf
6 small potatoes, peeled and diced
4 large carrots, scraped and diced
2 stalks celery, diced
1 large onion, chopped
1 (28-ounce) can tomatoes, undrained and chopped
1 (16-ounce) can tomato sauce
½ cup barley, uncooked
1 tablespoon chopped fresh parsley
1½ teaspoons salt
1 teaspoon dried whole basil
¼ teaspoon dried whole thyme
¼ teaspoon pepper

Place turkey carcass, water, and bay leaf in a large Dutch oven; bring to a boil. Cover, reduce heat, and simmer 2 hours. Remove carcass from broth, and pick meat from bones. Remove and discard bay leaf. Skim fat from broth, if necessary.

Return meat to broth; add potato and remaining ingredients. Cover and simmer 1 hour or until vegetables are tender. Yield: 3½ quarts.

Curried Turkey Salad, served on a bed of lettuce, is a dish that appeals to the eye as well as the palate.

Ham-Simmered Beans

2 pounds dried white, kidney, or pinto beans
3 quarts water
1 large smoked ham hock
2 large onions, chopped
3 large cloves garlic, minced
1 teaspoon salt
1 teaspoon dried whole thyme
1 teaspoon dried whole marjoram
3 bay leaves

Sort and wash beans; place in a large Dutch oven. Cover with water 2 inches above beans; let soak overnight. Drain beans, and return to Dutch oven. Add 3 quarts water and remaining ingredients to beans. Bring to a boil; cover, reduce heat, and simmer 1½ to 2 hours or until beans are tender. Remove ham hock and bay leaves. If desired, cut ham from hock and chop; return to beans. Yield: 16 cups.

TO STORE: Refrigerate remaining beans in a tightly covered container up to 5 days. Freeze in desired amounts in labeled airtight containers up to 6 months.

Hearty Sausage-Bean Soup

2 pounds bulk turkey sausage
1 large onion, chopped
4 cups Ham-Simmered Beans
3 cups water
2 (14½-ounce) cans tomatoes, undrained and chopped
2 medium potatoes, peeled and cubed
½ cup chopped green pepper
1 large bay leaf
½ teaspoon salt
½ teaspoon dried whole thyme
¼ teaspoon garlic powder
¼ teaspoon pepper

Cook sausage and onion in a large Dutch oven over medium heat until sausage is browned, stirring to crumble meat; drain. Stir in beans and remaining ingredients; bring to a boil. Cover, reduce heat, and simmer 1 hour. Remove bay leaf before serving. Yield: 14 cups.

Refried Beans

2 tablespoons vegetable oil
2 cups Ham-Simmered Beans
½ teaspoon garlic salt
½ cup (2 ounces) shredded Monterey Jack cheese with jalapeño peppers

Heat oil in a medium skillet; add beans and garlic salt. Mash beans. Add cheese, and cook over medium heat, stirring often, until cheese melts. Yield: 4 servings.

Warm up a winter evening with Hearty Sausage-Bean Soup. This soup teams nicely with a crisp green salad.

Tuna and Bean Salad

2 tablespoons olive oil
2 tablespoons red wine vinegar
2 teaspoons Dijon mustard
¼ teaspoon salt
⅛ teaspoon pepper
2 (6½-ounce) cans tuna in
  water, drained and flaked
2 cups Ham-Simmered Beans
1 medium-size sweet red
  pepper, cut into thin strips
½ small purple onion, thinly
  sliced and separated into rings
1 tablespoon minced fresh
  parsley
2 teaspoons minced fresh basil
Curly leaf lettuce

Combine oil, vinegar, mustard, salt, and pepper in a jar. Cover tightly, and shake vigorously. Chill thoroughly.

Combine tuna and next 5 ingredients. Pour chilled dressing over tuna mixture; toss gently. Serve on lettuce leaves. Yield: 5 cups.

Home-Style Baked Beans

8 slices bacon
2 medium onions, finely
  chopped
4 cups Ham-Simmered Beans
1 cup catsup
¼ cup firmly packed brown
  sugar
1 tablespoon plus 1 teaspoon
  spicy brown mustard
¼ teaspoon ground cloves
¼ teaspoon pepper

Cook bacon in a medium skillet until crisp; drain well, reserving 3 tablespoons drippings in skillet. Crumble bacon, and set aside.

Add onion to drippings; sauté over medium heat until tender. Stir in reserved bacon, beans, and remaining ingredients. Spoon bean mixture into a 2-quart casserole. Cover and bake at 400° for 30 minutes. Yield: 6 to 8 servings.

Your family will request Home-Style Baked Beans often because it's delicious; you will like it because it's so easy to prepare.

Basic Rice

4 cups water
1 teaspoon salt
2 cups long-grain rice, uncooked

Bring water and salt to a boil in a medium saucepan; add rice. Cover, reduce heat, and simmer 20 minutes or until rice is tender and water is absorbed. Yield: 6 cups.

TO STORE: Refrigerate remaining rice in a tightly covered container up to 1 week. Freeze in desired amounts in labeled airtight containers up to 1 month.

Pork Fried Rice

½ pound diced cooked pork
2 tablespoons vegetable oil, divided
⅛ teaspoon pepper
1 medium carrot, diced
1 stalk celery, sliced
½ cup chicken broth
¼ cup soy sauce, divided
3 cups cooked Basic Rice
2 eggs, lightly beaten
¼ teaspoon garlic powder
¼ teaspoon ground ginger
1 cup frozen English peas, thawed
½ cup sliced green onions

Sauté pork in 1 tablespoon oil in a large skillet over medium-high heat until pork is browned; remove from skillet with a slotted spoon. Sprinkle pork with pepper; set aside.

Sauté carrot and celery in remaining 1 tablespoon oil until crisp-tender (about 6 minutes). Add broth and 2 tablespoons soy sauce; cook until broth is reduced by half. Add rice, and cook until thoroughly heated.

Combine eggs, 1 tablespoon soy sauce, garlic powder, and ginger. Push rice mixture to sides of skillet, forming a well in center. Pour egg mixture into well, and cook until set, stirring occasionally. Stir rice mixture into eggs; add reserved pork, peas, green onions, and remaining 1 tablespoon soy sauce, stirring well. Cook 2 minutes or until thoroughly heated. Yield: 4 servings.

Rice Pudding

2 eggs, lightly beaten
1½ cups milk
¼ cup sugar
1 tablespoon butter or margarine, melted
½ teaspoon grated lemon rind
1 teaspoon lemon juice
1 teaspoon vanilla extract
⅛ teaspoon salt
2 cups cooked Basic Rice
⅓ cup raisins
2 tablespoons brown sugar
½ teaspoon ground cinnamon

Combine first 8 ingredients in a medium bowl; stir well. Stir in rice and raisins. Spoon mixture into a lightly greased 1-quart baking dish. Combine brown sugar and cinnamon; sprinkle over pudding. Bake at 325° for 1 hour or until set. Yield: 4 servings.

Pork Fried Rice gives leftover pork a delicious Oriental flavor.

Appetizers and Beverages

Some cooks find entertaining easy. If they are relaxed, it's because they know how to prepare for the event.

This chapter will help you to be a relaxed hostess and enjoy your own party because it allows you to anticipate social gatherings well in advance. Delectable morsels like Smoked Salmon Tarts and Chicken Cocktail Puffs will keep picture-perfect in the refrigerator or freezer. Quick back-ups for a casual bid to "stop by for drinks" include Delta Shrimp that can be cooked earlier and left to marinate until the cocktail hour. Hot Artichoke Spread and Tuna Spread take 10 to 15 minutes to put together the night before. Frozen Daiquiris and fruity White Sangría can be ready when the doorbell rings.

For the holidays or when you are expecting a houseful of guests, be prepared by keeping several pecan-studded Smoky Cheese Balls in the refrigerator and a batch of Crunchy Cheese Snacks in the freezer.

But don't reserve appetizers for company only. Serve them as festive meal-starters for the family, and turn the meal into a party. The appetizer soups fit well into everyday meals too. The soups are cool and summery; in contrast, the beverages Mocha-Cinnamon Cocoa and Hot Spiced Tea are winter-warmers—giving you choices for all seasons.

Entertain a hungry crowd during football season with these winning appetizers: Delta Shrimp (page 93), Crunchy Cheese Snacks (page 91), and White Sangría (page 98).

Smoked Salmon Tarts

4 (9-inch) refrigerated piecrusts
1½ cups half-and-half
4 eggs, beaten
¼ pound smoked salmon, chopped
½ cup (2 ounces) shredded Monterey Jack cheese
¼ cup minced green onions
½ teaspoon dried whole dillweed
¼ teaspoon salt
⅛ teaspoon pepper

Cut each piecrust into 14 circles, using a 2½-inch round cutter. Place rounds in greased miniature (1¾-inch) muffin cups; trim excess pastry.

Combine half-and-half and eggs in a medium bowl; stir with a wire whisk until well blended. Stir in salmon and remaining ingredients.

Spoon 1 tablespoon salmon mixture into each pastry shell. Bake at 375° for 25 to 30 minutes or until set. Remove from pans, and cool on wire racks.

TO STORE: Freeze tarts in a labeled airtight container up to 2 weeks.

TO SERVE: Thaw at room temperature. Place on baking sheets; cover and bake at 375° for 5 to 10 minutes or until hot. Yield: about 4 dozen.

Smoked Salmon Tarts look elegant when offered from a silver tray. Serve them anytime you want a dressy appetizer.

Party Pizzas

1 (10-ounce) package frozen chopped spinach, thawed and well drained
2 cups (8 ounces) shredded Monterey Jack cheese
½ cup mayonnaise
2 tablespoons sliced green onions
2 tablespoons chopped fresh chives
¼ teaspoon dried whole oregano
¼ teaspoon dried whole basil
⅛ teaspoon pepper
10 slices bacon, cooked and crumbled
30 slices party rye bread

Combine first 8 ingredients; stir well.

TO STORE: Refrigerate spinach mixture in a tightly covered container up to 3 days. Freeze cooked and crumbled bacon in a labeled airtight container up to 3 days.

TO SERVE: Place bread slices on a large baking sheet. Bake at 350° for 3 to 4 minutes on each side. Spread 1 tablespoon spinach mixture on one side of each bread slice; sprinkle evenly with bacon. Broil 6 inches from heat 3 to 4 minutes or until bubbly. Serve immediately. Yield: 2½ dozen.

Delta Shrimp

2 quarts water
½ large lemon, sliced
2½ pounds unpeeled large fresh shrimp
1 cup vegetable oil
2 tablespoons hot sauce
1½ teaspoons olive oil
1½ teaspoons minced garlic
1 teaspoon minced fresh parsley
¾ teaspoon salt
¾ teaspoon Old Bay seasoning
¾ teaspoon dried whole basil
¾ teaspoon dried whole oregano
¾ teaspoon dried whole thyme
Leaf lettuce
Commercial cocktail sauce

Bring water and lemon to a boil; add shrimp, and cook 3 to 5 minutes. Drain well; rinse with cold water. Peel and devein shrimp, leaving tails intact; place shrimp in a large bowl.
Combine vegetable oil and next 9 ingredients; stir with a wire whisk. Pour over shrimp; toss to coat shrimp.

TO STORE: Refrigerate in a tightly covered container up to 8 hours.

TO SERVE: Drain shrimp, and arrange in a large lettuce-lined bowl. Serve with cocktail sauce. Yield: 12 appetizer servings.

Frozen Daiquiris

2 (6-ounce) cans frozen limeade
   concentrate, thawed and
   undiluted
2 cups light rum
⅓ cup sifted powdered sugar
Ice cubes
Garnish: lime slices

Combine half of each of the first 3 ingredients in container of an electric blender. Process 30 seconds. Gradually add enough ice cubes to bring mixture to 4-cup level; blend until smooth. Pour mixture into a large freezer container. Repeat procedure with remaining half of ingredients.

TO STORE: Cover tightly, and freeze up to 1 month.

TO SERVE: Thaw 20 minutes or until mixture becomes slushy. Stir and serve immediately. Garnish, if desired. Yield: 9 cups.

Frozen Strawberry Daiquiris

1 (6-ounce) can frozen limeade
  concentrate, thawed and
  undiluted
1 cup light rum
¼ cup sifted powdered sugar
1 cup sliced fresh strawberries
Ice cubes
Garnish: fresh strawberries

Combine first 4 ingredients in container of an electric blender. Process 30 seconds. Gradually add enough ice cubes to bring mixture to 4-cup level; blend until smooth.

TO STORE: Freeze beverage in a labeled airtight container up to 1 month.

TO SERVE: Thaw 20 minutes or until mixture becomes slushy. Stir and serve immediately. Garnish, if desired. Yield: about 4 cups.

Frozen Peach Daiquiris: Substitute 2 medium peaches, peeled and chopped, for strawberries. Garnish with fresh peach wedges, if desired.

Frozen Pineapple Daiquiris: Substitute 1 cup fresh pineapple chunks for strawberries. Garnish with fresh pineapple chunks, if desired.

Special Iced Coffee

3 cups boiling water
2 tablespoons instant coffee
  granules
4 (3-inch) sticks cinnamon
6 whole cloves
6 whole allspice
2 (3- x ¼-inch) strips orange
  rind
2 (3- x ¼-inch) strips lemon
  rind
⅓ cup Kahlúa or other
  coffee-flavored liqueur
⅓ cup amaretto or other
  almond-flavored liqueur
8 cups cold coffee
Garnishes: sweetened whipped
  cream and orange rind curls

Combine first 7 ingredients; cover and let stand at room temperature 2 hours. Strain and discard spices and rind. Pour liquid evenly into 2 ice cube trays.

TO STORE: Freeze coffee mixture until firm; transfer frozen cubes to a labeled zip-top heavy-duty plastic bag. Freeze up to 1 month.

TO SERVE: For each serving, place 3 coffee cubes in a tall glass. Add 2 teaspoons each of Kahlúa and amaretto. Add 1 cup cold coffee to each glass, stirring well. Garnish, if desired. Yield: 8 servings.

Take the heat out of a summer afternoon by sipping frosty Frozen Daiquiris or Frozen Strawberry Daiquiris in the shade.

Main Dishes

What distinguishes main courses from other foods is that you almost always have to serve one. And these dishes take some thought if you want to provide a variety of meals.

Many of the entrées in this chapter can be assembled quickly the night before cooking; some are left to marinate, while others can be frozen. With many of the recipes for meats and poultry, advance preparation actually improves results because the additional time can help to tenderize and allow seasonings to permeate and blend.

Chicken marinates well, but not for more than a day; after cooking, it will retain better flavor in the freezer if submerged in a sauce. Beef and pork are sturdier; they can be marinated up to two days. Large cuts of lamb improve in flavor if marinated several days before cooking. Seafood is the most fragile fare; only very firm types, such as shrimp or salmon, should be marinated more than a couple of hours. Use heavy-duty zip-top plastic bags for easiest marinating; just by turning the bag you can turn the food over for even penetration of the marinade.

Although most fully cooked main courses can be cooled in the refrigerator and then frozen, some guidelines apply. It is best to omit vegetables such as potatoes, mushrooms, and peas from combination dishes, because they do not freeze well. These vegetables will retain better color, texture, and nutrient content if added during reheating instead of prior to freezing.

For the same reason, it is also best to refrigerate or freeze seafood soups and stews without the seafood, which can be added during reheating. For safety's sake, do not freeze stuffed poultry, and do not defrost poultry at room temperature—whether cooked or uncooked.

Stuffed with fresh asparagus and green onions, Oriental Flank Steak Rolls (page 102) is an impressive make-ahead main dish.

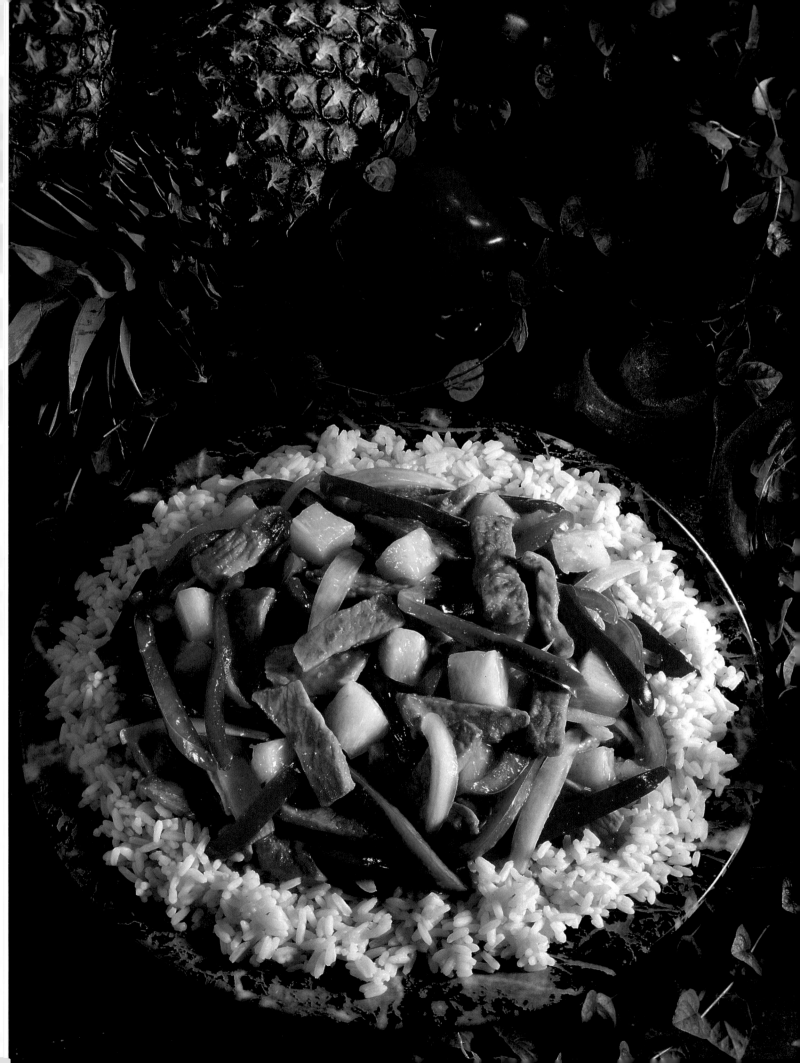

Sweet-and-Sour Pork

1 (20-ounce) can pineapple
  chunks, undrained
1½ pounds boneless pork,
  trimmed
1 tablespoon vegetable oil
½ cup water
⅓ cup vinegar
¼ cup firmly packed brown
  sugar
1 tablespoon soy sauce
½ teaspoon salt
2 tablespoons cornstarch
½ cup water
1 medium onion, cut into thin
  wedges
1 small green pepper, cut into
  strips
1 small sweet red pepper, cut
  into strips
Hot cooked rice

Drain pineapple, reserving juice. Refrigerate pineapple chunks in a tightly covered container. Set juice aside.

Partially freeze pork; slice diagonally across grain into 2- x 1- x ¼-inch strips. Sauté pork strips in hot oil in a large skillet until browned; drain. Stir in reserved pineapple juice, ½ cup water, and next 4 ingredients. Cover, reduce heat to low, and simmer 30 minutes, stirring occasionally.

Combine cornstarch and ½ cup water, stirring until smooth. Add to pork mixture, stirring constantly; cook over medium-low heat 2 minutes or until sauce is clear and thickened. Cool.

TO STORE: Refrigerate in a tightly covered container up to 2 days.

TO SERVE: Cook pork mixture in a large skillet over medium heat until simmering, stirring occasionally. Stir in onion, peppers, and reserved pineapple chunks; cover and cook, stirring occasionally, 2 minutes or until vegetables are crisp-tender and thoroughly heated. Serve with hot cooked rice. Yield: 4 to 6 servings.

Italian Stuffed Peppers

4 medium-size green peppers
½ pound hot Italian sausage
½ pound ground chuck
1 cup chopped onion
1 clove garlic, minced
1 cup cooked rice
1 (8-ounce) can tomato sauce
1 (2¼-ounce) can sliced ripe
  olives, drained
½ teaspoon salt
½ teaspoon dried whole basil
½ teaspoon pepper
½ cup (2 ounces) shredded
  Cheddar cheese

Cut off tops of green peppers, and remove seeds. Cook peppers 5 minutes in boiling water to cover; drain peppers, and set aside.

Cook sausage, ground chuck, onion, and garlic in a large skillet until meat is browned, stirring to crumble meat; drain. Stir in rice and next 5 ingredients. Stuff peppers with meat mixture, and place in a lightly greased 8-inch square baking dish.

TO STORE: Cover and refrigerate up to 24 hours.

TO SERVE: Bake, uncovered, at 350° for 30 minutes. Sprinkle tops of peppers with cheese; bake an additional 5 minutes or until cheese melts. Yield: 4 servings.

Sweet-and-Sour Pork is colorful and attractive. Served over hot cooked rice, this is a filling one-dish meal.

Spaghetti Squash Italiano

1½ pounds bulk pork sausage
1 cup sliced fresh mushrooms
½ cup sliced green onions
1 clove garlic, minced
2 (15-ounce) cans tomato sauce
2 medium tomatoes, peeled and chopped
2 tablespoons dried whole basil
1 tablespoon dried whole oregano
½ teaspoon pepper
1 (3-pound) spaghetti squash
2 cups (8 ounces) shredded Cheddar cheese

Cook sausage in a large skillet until browned, stirring to crumble. Drain sausage, reserving 2 tablespoons drippings; set sausage aside. Sauté mushrooms, onions, and garlic in reserved pan drippings until tender. Stir in sausage, tomato sauce, and next 4 ingredients. Bring to a boil; reduce heat, and simmer, uncovered, 15 to 20 minutes, stirring occasionally. Cool.

TO STORE: Refrigerate sauce in a tightly covered container up to 3 days. Freeze in a labeled airtight container up to 2 weeks.

TO SERVE: Thaw sauce in refrigerator. Wash squash; pierce with a fork several times. Place squash in a shallow baking dish. Bake at 350° for 1 hour or until squash yields to pressure. Let cool to touch.
Cut squash in half lengthwise; remove and discard seeds. Using a fork, remove spaghetti-like strands from squash. Place half of squash in a 13- x 9- x 2-inch baking dish; pour half of sauce over squash. Repeat layers. Spread cheese evenly over top. Bake at 350° for 30 to 35 minutes or until bubbly. Yield: 6 to 8 servings.

Herbed Leg of Lamb

1 cup olive oil
½ cup balsamic vinegar
½ cup chopped onion
2 tablespoons Dijon mustard
6 fresh parsley sprigs
3 cloves garlic, crushed
2 bay leaves
½ teaspoon salt
½ teaspoon dried whole oregano
½ teaspoon dried whole basil
½ teaspoon dried whole rosemary
½ teaspoon dried whole dillweed
½ teaspoon dried whole marjoram
½ teaspoon pepper
1 (5- to 7-pound) boneless leg of lamb, rolled and tied
Commercial mint jelly (optional)

Combine first 14 ingredients; stir well. Place lamb in a large shallow dish; pour marinade over lamb.

TO STORE: Cover and refrigerate up to 2 days, turning occasionally.

TO SERVE: Remove lamb from marinade; discard marinade. Place lamb on rack in a large roasting pan. Insert meat thermometer into thickest part of lamb, making sure it does not touch fat or bone. Bake at 325° for 2½ to 3 hours or until thermometer registers 140° (rare) or 160° (medium). Let stand 10 minutes before carving. Serve with mint jelly, if desired. Yield: 8 to 10 servings.

Take a break from ordinary pasta by serving Spaghetti Squash Italiano. The spaghetti-like strands of this vegetable give this family favorite a new twist.

Fiesta Chicken Rolls

8 chicken breast halves, skinned and boned
¼ cup (1 ounce) shredded Cheddar cheese
1 (3-ounce) package cream cheese, softened
2 tablespoons butter or margarine, softened
2 tablespoons chopped green chiles
2 tablespoons grated onion
¼ teaspoon salt
⅛ teaspoon black pepper
1¾ cups bite-size Cheddar cheese crackers, crushed
1 teaspoon chili powder
¼ teaspoon ground cumin
¼ teaspoon ground red pepper
⅛ teaspoon garlic powder
¼ cup butter or margarine, melted

Place chicken between 2 sheets of heavy-duty plastic wrap; flatten to ¼-inch thickness, using a meat mallet or rolling pin. Set aside. Combine Cheddar cheese and next 6 ingredients in a small bowl; stir well.

Spoon cheese mixture evenly over center of each chicken breast half. Roll up jellyroll fashion, starting with short end; secure with wooden picks.

Combine cracker crumbs, chili powder, cumin, red pepper, and garlic powder in a small bowl; stir well. Dip chicken in melted butter; dredge in crumb mixture. Place seam side down in a 13- x 9- x 2-inch baking dish.

TO STORE: Cover and refrigerate up to 24 hours.

TO SERVE: Bake, uncovered, at 400° for 20 to 25 minutes or until done. Remove wooden picks before serving. Yield: 8 servings.

Company Chicken-Artichoke Bake

¼ cup butter or margarine
6 chicken breast halves, skinned and boned
1 cup chopped onion
1 clove garlic, minced
3 tablespoons all-purpose flour
¼ teaspoon salt
1¼ cups Chablis or other dry white wine
1 cup chicken broth
1 (3-ounce) package cream cheese
1 (14-ounce) can artichoke hearts, drained and halved
½ cup sliced natural almonds, toasted

Melt butter in a large skillet over medium heat. Add chicken, and cook 5 minutes on each side or until browned. Remove chicken from skillet, reserving pan drippings; place chicken in a 2-quart casserole. Set aside.

Sauté onion and garlic in reserved pan drippings until tender. Add flour and salt, stirring until smooth. Cook 1 minute, stirring constantly. Gradually add wine and broth; cook over medium heat, stirring constantly, until mixture is thickened and bubbly. Add cream cheese, stirring until cheese melts. Remove from heat; set aside.

Arrange halved artichoke hearts over chicken. Spoon cream cheese mixture over chicken and artichokes. Cool.

TO STORE: Cover and refrigerate up to 24 hours.

TO SERVE: Bake, covered, at 350° for 45 to 50 minutes or until bubbly. Sprinkle with toasted almonds. Yield: 4 to 6 servings.

Entertaining is easy with Company Chicken-Artichoke Bake. White wine enhances the flavor of this special dish.

Chicken Romano

8 chicken breast halves, skinned
and boned
2 tablespoons butter or
margarine, melted
2 tablespoons olive oil
½ pound sweet Italian sausage
½ cup finely chopped onion
½ cup sliced fresh mushrooms
1 clove garlic, minced
1 (6-ounce) can tomato paste
1 cup Chablis
¼ cup water
1 teaspoon dried whole basil
½ teaspoon dried whole
oregano
¼ teaspoon dried whole
marjoram
¼ teaspoon salt
¼ teaspoon pepper
½ cup (2 ounces) shredded
mozzarella cheese

Sauté chicken in butter and olive oil in a large skillet over medium heat until browned on both sides. Transfer chicken to a lightly greased 13- x 9- x 2-inch baking dish, reserving drippings in skillet.

Cook sausage, onion, mushrooms, and garlic in reserved drippings until meat is browned, stirring to crumble meat. Drain. Return sausage mixture to skillet; stir in tomato paste and next 7 ingredients. Bring to a boil; reduce heat, and simmer, uncovered, 15 minutes, stirring occasionally. Pour sauce over chicken.

TO STORE: Cover and refrigerate up to 24 hours.

TO SERVE: Bake, covered, at 350° for 25 minutes. Uncover and bake 20 minutes or until thoroughly heated. Sprinkle with cheese, and bake an additional 5 minutes or until cheese melts. Yield: 8 servings.

Country Chicken Pot Pies

1 cup chopped onion
1 cup chopped celery
1 cup chopped carrot
⅓ cup butter or margarine,
melted
½ cup all-purpose flour
2 cups chicken broth
1 cup half-and-half
4 cups chopped cooked chicken
1 cup frozen English peas,
thawed
1 teaspoon salt
¼ teaspoon pepper
Basic Pastry

Sauté first 3 ingredients in butter in a skillet over medium heat until tender. Add flour; stir until smooth. Cook 1 minute, stirring constantly. Add chicken broth and half-and-half; cook, stirring constantly, until thickened and bubbly. Stir in chicken, peas, salt, and pepper.

Divide Basic Pastry into 8 equal portions. Roll 4 portions of pastry to 10-inch circles on a floured surface. Place in four 6-inch disposable pie pans. Divide chicken mixture over pastry in pans. Roll remaining 4 portions of pastry to 7-inch circles on a floured surface. Place pastry circles over filling; fold edges under and flute. Cut slits in tops to allow steam to escape.

TO STORE: Cover tightly, and freeze up to 1 month.

TO SERVE: Bake, uncovered, at 400° for 1 hour or until crust is golden brown. Yield: 4 servings.

Basic Pastry

4 cups all-purpose flour
2 teaspoons salt
1½ cups plus 1 tablespoon
shortening
⅓ to ½ cup cold water

Combine flour and salt; cut in shortening with a pastry blender until mixture resembles coarse meal. Sprinkle cold water (1 tablespoon at a time) over surface; stir with a fork until dry ingredients are moistened. Shape into a ball; chill. Yield: pastry for four 6-inch pies.

Country Chicken Pot Pies are filled with chicken and vegetables and topped with a flaky homemade crust.

Grilled Salmon Steaks

½ cup lemon juice
2 tablespoons minced fresh dillweed
2 tablespoons olive oil
½ teaspoon salt
¼ teaspoon ground white pepper
4 (8-ounce) salmon steaks (about 1-inch thick)
Tarragon-Dill Mayonnaise
Garnishes: lemon slices and fresh dillweed sprigs

Combine first 5 ingredients in a jar. Cover tightly, and shake vigorously. Set aside.

Arrange salmon steaks in a shallow baking dish. Pour marinade over steaks, turning to coat both sides.

TO STORE: Cover and refrigerate up to 8 hours, turning steaks occasionally.

TO SERVE: Remove steaks from marinade, reserving marinade. Pour marinade into a small saucepan. Bring to a boil over medium heat; reduce heat, and simmer 5 minutes. Grill steaks over hot coals 7 to 8 minutes on each side or until salmon flakes easily when tested with a fork, basting frequently with reserved marinade. Serve with Tarragon-Dill Mayonnaise. Garnish, if desired. Yield: 4 servings.

Tarragon-Dill Mayonnaise

½ cup mayonnaise
½ cup sour cream
1 tablespoon Dijon mustard
1 teaspoon white wine Worcestershire sauce
1 clove garlic, crushed
1 teaspoon dried whole tarragon
½ teaspoon dried whole dillweed
¼ teaspoon seasoned salt
Dash of ground white pepper

Combine all ingredients in a small bowl, stirring well.

TO STORE: Refrigerate in a tightly covered container up to 3 days. Yield: 1 cup.

Shrimp and Vegetable Kabobs

1½ pounds unpeeled medium-size fresh shrimp
1 (8-ounce) bottle Italian salad dressing
¼ cup grated Parmesan cheese
¼ cup water
½ teaspoon crushed red pepper
8 boiling onions
16 small fresh mushrooms
2 small zucchini, cut into 1-inch slices
1 large sweet red pepper, cut into 1-inch pieces

Peel shrimp, leaving tails intact. Place shrimp in a zip-top heavy-duty plastic bag. Combine salad dressing and next 3 ingredients; stir well, and pour over shrimp.

TO STORE: Refrigerate shrimp up to 24 hours, turning occasionally.

TO SERVE: Parboil onions 5 minutes; drain well, and set aside. Remove shrimp from marinade, reserving marinade. Pour marinade into a small saucepan. Bring to a boil over medium heat; reduce heat, and simmer 5 minutes, stirring frequently.

Alternate shrimp and vegetables on eight 12-inch skewers. Grill kabobs over medium-hot coals 4 minutes on each side or to desired degree of doneness, turning and basting frequently with marinade. Yield: 4 servings.

Shrimp and Vegetable Kabobs are a marvelous entrée from the grill.

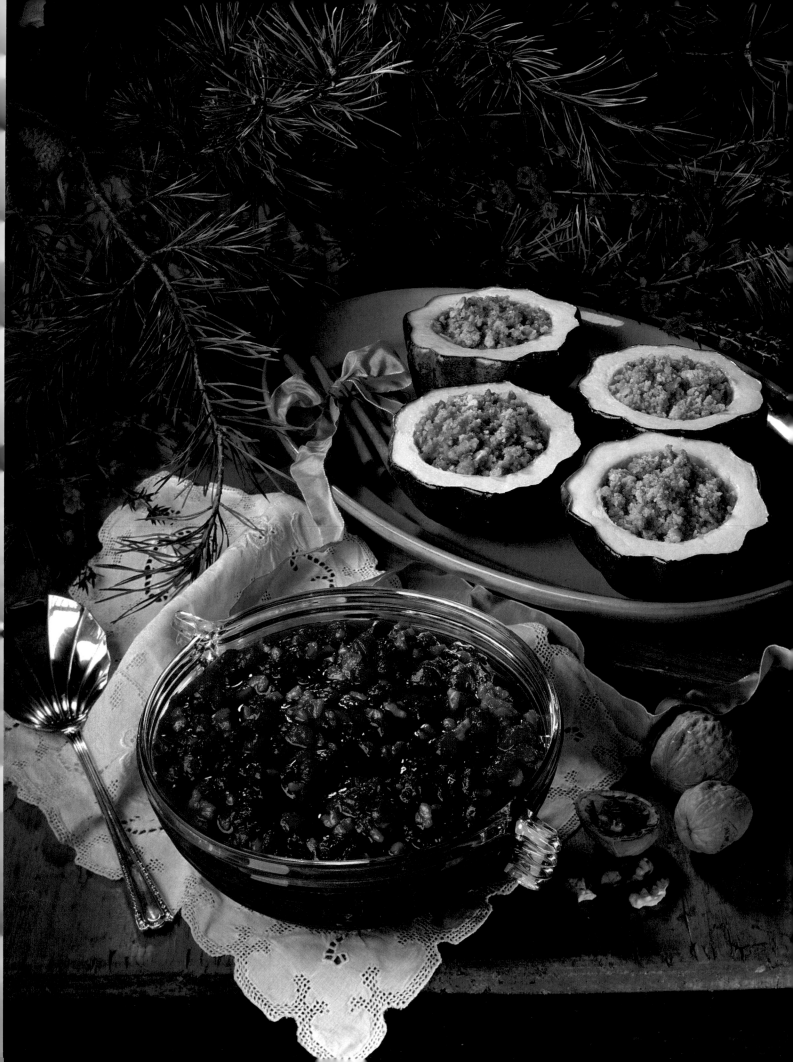

Accompaniments

Do-ahead accompaniments fall into three basic categories. First, there are breads and pasta or rice dishes. Some of the breads keep as refrigerated or frozen dough, such as Angel Biscuits and Refrigerator Potato Rolls, and some are baked, frozen, and ready to reheat, such as Country Corn Cakes and Wild Rice-Pecan Muffins. The rice and the pasta dishes, such as Broccoli-Rice Combo and Noodles Romanoff, may be prepared a couple of days ahead and can be used in place of a bread in the meal. Second, there are recipes that must be refrigerated to congeal or to allow flavors to blend, such as Congealed Beet Salad Piquant, Refrigerator Pickled Vegetable Medley, and Gingered Summer Fruit Compote. Third, there are the side dishes that are prepared in two stages. These include casseroles like Italian Green Bean and Artichoke Casserole, which can be assembled one day and baked the next, and Zesty Stuffed Onions, filled with a flavorful mixture one day and baked the next day.

There are also foods that take more time to prepare but keep well, like Smoky Red Beans and Rice. The bean mixture simmers for 2 hours initially. When ready to serve, reheat the bean mixture while the rice cooks.

For big parties, consider the salads and marinated vegetables that will hold up as well on a buffet table as they do in the refrigerator. The recipes for these dishes can be doubled or tripled easily. The vegetable salads are great for picnics and covered-dish suppers too.

Holiday meals will be less hectic when you serve festive made-ahead side dishes such as Pecan-Kissed Squash (page 143) and Baked Cranberry-Orange Sauce (page 133).

Herbed Bread Italiano

1 (16-ounce) loaf unsliced
  Italian bread
¼ cup butter or margarine,
  softened
¼ cup finely chopped pepperoni
3 tablespoons grated Parmesan
  cheese
1 clove garlic, crushed
1 tablespoon minced fresh
  parsley
½ teaspoon dried whole basil
½ teaspoon dried whole
  oregano

Cut bread diagonally into 1-inch slices, cutting to but not through bottom of loaf. Combine butter and remaining ingredients; spread on cut sides of bread.

TO STORE: Wrap in heavy-duty aluminum foil. Refrigerate up to 2 days. Label and freeze up to 2 weeks.

TO SERVE: Thaw loaf in refrigerator. Loosen foil. Bake at 400° for 20 minutes or until bread is thoroughly heated. Yield: 1 loaf.

Poppy Seed-Dill Biscuits

2 cups all-purpose flour
1 tablespoon baking powder
1 teaspoon salt
1 teaspoon dried whole dillweed
⅓ cup shortening
¾ cup milk
Poppy seeds

Combine first 4 ingredients in a large bowl; cut in shortening with a pastry blender until mixture resembles coarse meal. Add milk to mixture, stirring until dry ingredients are moistened. Turn dough out onto a lightly floured surface, and knead 4 or 5 times.

Roll dough to ½-inch thickness; cut with a 2½-inch biscuit cutter. Place biscuits ½ inch apart on a lightly greased baking sheet. Brush tops of biscuits lightly with water; sprinkle with poppy seeds, gently pressing seeds into biscuits.

TO STORE: Cover tightly, and freeze 2 hours or until firm. Place frozen biscuits in a zip-top heavy-duty plastic bag. Freeze up to 1 week.

TO SERVE: Place frozen biscuits on an ungreased baking sheet. Bake at 425° for 20 to 25 minutes or until golden brown. Yield: 9 biscuits.

Country Corn Cakes are a delightful, old-fashioned way to round out a menu that features fresh summer vegetables.

Country Corn Cakes

1 (10-ounce) package frozen
    whole kernel corn, thawed
2 tablespoons finely chopped
    onion
2 tablespoons finely chopped
    celery
1 (2-ounce) jar diced pimiento,
    drained
1½ cups buttermilk
1 egg, lightly beaten
2 tablespoons butter or
    margarine, melted
¼ teaspoon salt
1¾ cups self-rising cornmeal
¼ cup vegetable oil, divided

Finely chop ½ cup corn. Combine chopped and un-chopped corn, onion, and next 6 ingredients in a medium bowl; stir well. Gradually add cornmeal, stirring just until moistened.

Heat 2 tablespoons oil in a large skillet over medium-high heat. Pour ¼ cup batter into skillet for each corn cake, cooking 3 or 4 cakes at a time. Cook 4 to 5 minutes on each side or until browned. Drain cakes on paper towels. Repeat procedure using remaining batter and adding oil to skillet, if necessary. Cool.

TO STORE: Refrigerate corn cakes in a tightly covered container up to 2 days. Freeze corn cakes in a labeled airtight container up to 1 month.

TO SERVE: Place cakes on ungreased baking sheets. Bake at 350° for 10 to 12 minutes or until thoroughly heated. Yield: 14 corn cakes.

Wild Rice-Pecan Muffins

1 cup whole wheat flour
½ cup all-purpose flour
1 teaspoon baking powder
1 teaspoon baking soda
½ teaspoon salt
3 tablespoons brown sugar
1 egg, lightly beaten
1 (8-ounce) carton plain yogurt
¼ cup vegetable oil
½ teaspoon vanilla extract
½ cup cooked wild rice
¼ cup chopped pecans, toasted

Combine first 6 ingredients in a large bowl; make a well in center of mixture. Combine egg, yogurt, oil, and vanilla; add to dry ingredients, stirring just until moistened. Fold in rice and pecans.

Spoon batter into greased muffin pans, filling two-thirds full. Bake at 400° for 18 to 20 minutes or until golden brown. Remove from pans immediately. Cool on wire racks.

TO STORE: Freeze muffins in a labeled airtight container up to 2 weeks.

TO SERVE: Thaw at room temperature. Serve muffins warm or at room temperature. Yield: 1 dozen.

Angel Biscuits

1 package dry yeast
¼ cup warm water (105° to 115°)
2 cups buttermilk
5 cups all-purpose flour
1 tablespoon baking powder
1 teaspoon baking soda
1 teaspoon salt
¼ cup sugar
1 cup shortening

Combine yeast and warm water; let stand 5 minutes. Add buttermilk to yeast mixture, and set aside.

Combine flour and next 4 ingredients in a large bowl; cut in shortening with a pastry blender until mixture resembles coarse meal. Add buttermilk mixture, stirring just until dry ingredients are moistened. Turn dough out onto a lightly floured surface, and knead 4 or 5 times. Shape dough into a ball.

TO STORE: Refrigerate in a tightly covered container up to 1 week.

TO SERVE: Roll dough to ½-inch thickness; cut with a 2-inch biscuit cutter. Place on lightly greased baking sheets. Bake at 400° for 13 to 15 minutes or until golden brown. Yield: 4½ dozen.

Refrigerator Potato Rolls

1 medium potato, peeled and quartered
1 package dry yeast
1 teaspoon sugar
¼ cup butter or margarine, melted
2 tablespoons shortening, melted
¼ cup honey
1 egg, lightly beaten
1½ teaspoons salt
3 to 3½ cups all-purpose flour, divided

Cook potato in boiling water to cover 15 minutes or until tender. Drain, reserving ½ cup liquid; set potato aside. Cool reserved liquid to 105° to 115°; stir in yeast and sugar. Let stand 5 minutes.

Mash enough potato to measure ½ cup; place in a large mixing bowl. Add butter, shortening, honey, egg, salt, yeast mixture, and 1¼ cups flour. Beat at medium speed of an electric mixer 2 minutes. Gradually stir in enough remaining flour to make a soft dough.

Turn dough out onto a well-floured surface, and knead until smooth and elastic (6 to 8 minutes). Divide dough in half. Shape each half into 12 balls, and place in 2 greased 8-inch round pans.

TO STORE: Cover and refrigerate up to 4 days.

TO SERVE: Cover and let rise in a warm place (85°), free from drafts, 1 hour and 30 minutes to 1 hour and 45 minutes or until doubled in bulk. Bake at 375° for 15 to 20 minutes or until golden. Yield: 2 dozen.

Your family and friends will rave when you serve freshly baked Refrigerator Potato Rolls.

Broccoli-Rice Combo

1 (6-ounce) package long-grain and wild rice mix
1 (10¾-ounce) can cream of chicken soup, undiluted
1 (10-ounce) package frozen chopped broccoli, thawed
1 (8-ounce) can sliced water chestnuts, drained
1 cup (4 ounces) shredded Cheddar cheese
½ cup sliced celery
½ cup chopped onion
½ cup milk
1 (2-ounce) jar sliced pimiento, drained
½ cup coarsely crushed chow mein noodles

Cook rice according to package directions, using 2 cups water. Combine rice and next 8 ingredients, stirring well. Spoon mixture into a lightly greased 2-quart casserole.

TO STORE: Cover and refrigerate up to 2 days.

TO SERVE: Bake, uncovered, at 350° for 35 to 40 minutes. Sprinkle with crushed chow mein noodles, and bake an additional 5 minutes. Yield: 4 to 6 servings.

Noodles Romanoff

1 (8-ounce) package medium-size curly egg noodles
1 cup small-curd cottage cheese
1 (8-ounce) carton sour cream
½ cup sliced ripe olives
½ cup sliced green onions
1 teaspoon Worcestershire sauce
½ teaspoon salt
⅛ teaspoon ground red pepper
½ cup (2 ounces) shredded Cheddar cheese

Cook noodles according to package directions, omitting salt. Drain well. Combine noodles, cottage cheese, and next 6 ingredients, stirring well. Spoon mixture into a lightly greased 11- x 7- x 1½-inch baking dish.

TO STORE: Cover and refrigerate up to 2 days.

TO SERVE: Bake, uncovered, at 350° for 30 to 35 minutes. Sprinkle with shredded Cheddar cheese, and bake an additional 5 minutes or until cheese melts. Yield: 6 to 8 servings.

The rich, creamy texture and cheesy flavor of Noodles Romanoff will make it a popular addition to many meals.

Festive Raspberry Ribbon Salad

1 (3-ounce) package
    raspberry-flavored gelatin
¾ cup boiling water
1 (10-ounce) package frozen
    raspberries in syrup, thawed
    and undrained
1 (8-ounce) can crushed
    pineapple, undrained
¼ cup chopped pecans
1 (8-ounce) carton sour cream
Curly leaf lettuce

Dissolve gelatin in boiling water in a large bowl; add raspberries, pineapple, and pecans, stirring until blended.

Spoon half of raspberry mixture into a lightly oiled 8-inch square dish; chill until firm. Store remaining raspberry mixture at room temperature.

Spread sour cream evenly over congealed gelatin layer. Spoon reserved gelatin mixture over sour cream.

TO STORE: Cover salad, and refrigerate until firm and up to 2 days.

TO SERVE: Cut salad into squares, and serve on lettuce leaves. Yield: 9 servings.

Gingered Summer Fruit Compote

1 tablespoon sugar
2 teaspoons cornstarch
½ teaspoon ground ginger
1 cup pineapple juice
1½ cups fresh pineapple chunks
1½ cups fresh strawberries,
    hulled
1 cup sliced fresh peaches
1 cup fresh blueberries
Garnish: fresh mint sprigs

Combine first 3 ingredients in a small saucepan; gradually add pineapple juice, stirring until smooth. Bring mixture to a boil over medium heat; boil 1 minute, stirring constantly. Remove from heat; cool.

Combine pineapple, strawberries, peaches, and blueberries in a large bowl. Pour sauce over fruit; toss gently.

TO STORE: Refrigerate in a tightly covered container up to 8 hours.

TO SERVE: Spoon fruit mixture into individual serving bowls. Garnish, if desired. Yield: 5 cups.

Gingered Summer Fruit Compote stars as a colorful addition to any menu. For a finishing touch, garnish individual servings with fresh mint sprigs.

Frozen Individual Waldorf Salads

1 (8¼-ounce) can crushed
  pineapple, undrained
2 eggs, lightly beaten
½ cup sugar
2½ cups chopped apple
¼ cup lemon juice
⅔ cup chopped celery
⅔ cup chopped walnuts
⅔ cup miniature marshmallows
¼ cup mayonnaise
1 cup whipping cream, whipped

Drain pineapple, reserving juice. Set pineapple aside. Combine reserved pineapple juice, eggs, and sugar in a large saucepan. Cook over medium heat, stirring constantly, until thickened and smooth. Remove from heat; cool slightly.

Combine chopped apple and lemon juice in a small bowl; add to thickened mixture. Add reserved pineapple, celery, and next 3 ingredients, stirring well. Fold in whipped cream. Spoon salad into paper-lined muffin pans, filling each three-fourths full.

TO STORE: Cover and freeze until firm. Remove salads from muffin pans, and place in large zip-top heavy-duty plastic bags. Freeze up to 1 month.

TO SERVE: Let stand at room temperature 5 minutes before serving. Serve immediately. Yield: 18 servings.

Eight-Layer Salad

1 small head iceberg lettuce,
  torn into bite-size pieces
1 small head romaine lettuce,
  torn into bite-size pieces
½ pound bacon, cooked and
  crumbled
1 small purple onion, chopped
1 (10-ounce) package frozen
  English peas, thawed
1 medium-size sweet red
  pepper, chopped
1 (8-ounce) can sliced water
  chestnuts, drained
1 cup (4 ounces) shredded
  sharp Cheddar cheese
¾ cup mayonnaise
¾ cup sour cream
Garnish: sweet red pepper rings

Layer first 8 ingredients in order listed in a large salad bowl. Combine mayonnaise and sour cream, stirring well; spread over top of salad, sealing to edge of bowl.

TO STORE: Cover and refrigerate up to 24 hours.

TO SERVE: Garnish, if desired. Yield: 12 servings.

Eight-Layer Salad, with a variety of crisp, flavorful ingredients, offers cool refreshment for summer dining.

Company Potato Rosettes

2 medium potatoes, peeled and
  quartered
½ cup (2 ounces) shredded
  sharp Cheddar cheese
1 egg, lightly beaten
2 tablespoons minced green
  onions
2 tablespoons sour cream
½ teaspoon salt
¼ teaspoon ground white
  pepper
1 (2-ounce) jar diced pimiento,
  drained and minced

Cook potatoes in boiling water to cover 15 minutes or until tender; drain. Mash potatoes in a medium bowl. Add cheese and next 5 ingredients, stirring to blend. Stir in pimiento. Cool slightly.

Spoon potato mixture into a decorating bag fitted with a large star tip. Pipe mixture into 12 rosettes on a wax paper-lined baking sheet.

TO STORE: Cover and freeze 3 hours or until firm. Place rosettes in a zip-top heavy-duty freezer bag. Freeze up to 1 month.

TO SERVE: Place frozen rosettes on a lightly greased baking sheet. Bake at 350° for 25 to 30 minutes or until lightly browned. Yield: 6 servings.

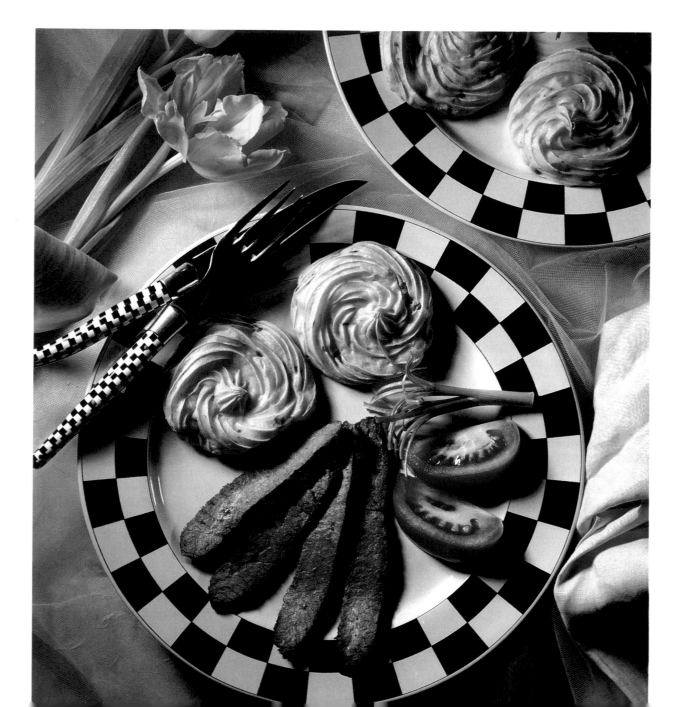

Pecan-Kissed Squash

2 large acorn squash (about 1¼
  pounds each)
20 round buttery crackers,
  crushed
½ cup coarsely chopped pecans
¼ cup butter or margarine,
  melted
¼ cup firmly packed brown
  sugar
¼ teaspoon pumpkin pie spice

Cut squash in half crosswise; remove and discard seeds. Place squash halves, cut side up, in a shallow baking dish. Combine cracker crumbs and remaining ingredients, stirring well. Spoon mixture evenly into squash cavities.

TO STORE: Cover and refrigerate up to 24 hours.

TO SERVE: Pour hot water to a depth of ½ inch into dish with squash. Bake at 350° for 1 hour or until squash is tender. Yield: 4 servings.

Curried Vegetable Combo

2 cups cauliflower flowerets
2 cups scraped, sliced carrot
2 cups sliced celery
½ cup chopped onion
1 (10¾-ounce) can cream of
  chicken soup, undiluted
⅓ cup mayonnaise
½ teaspoon salt
½ teaspoon curry powder
¼ teaspoon ground coriander
⅛ teaspoon ground ginger
½ cup (2 ounces) shredded
  Cheddar cheese
½ cup soft breadcrumbs
2 tablespoons butter or
  margarine, melted

Cook cauliflower, carrot, celery, and onion in a small amount of boiling water 3 minutes or until crisp-tender. Drain and set aside.
Combine soup and next 5 ingredients in a large bowl, stirring well. Stir in vegetables. Spoon mixture into a 1½-quart casserole.

TO STORE: Cover and refrigerate up to 24 hours.

TO SERVE: Combine cheese, breadcrumbs, and butter; sprinkle mixture over casserole. Bake, uncovered, at 350° for 30 to 35 minutes or until bubbly. Yield: 4 to 6 servings.

Plain potatoes become exciting when piped into pretty swirls for Company Potato Rosettes.

Desserts

With a little planning, you can always have dessert on hand for a birthday, an anniversary, a holiday celebration, or a late-night craving. The selections are as delicious as Raspberry-Almond Chocolate Cake, Sour Cream-Streusel Pound Cake, Favorite Apple Pie, or Old-Fashioned Vanilla Ice Cream.

Keep these points in mind when preparing make-ahead desserts. It is better to freeze cakes without the frosting. Wrap a cooled sheet cake in heavy-duty aluminum foil, or place cake layers in zip-top heavy-duty plastic bags and freeze. Defrost the cake in the wrapping at room temperature, allowing about 1 hour for cake layers and up to 3 hours for a sheet cake to thaw. Frost the cake when you are ready to serve it.

Cookies generally freeze well. Bar cookies may be cut and frozen individually. Or bake and freeze bar cookies in disposable aluminum pans; cut into bars or squares after thawing.

Pie pastry will be crisper if pies are frozen unbaked. Wrap the pie with heavy-duty aluminum foil, and place in a box or a large freezer bag for best protection.

Homemade ice creams and sherbets made with a cooked custard base will keep 2 to 4 weeks in the freezer if the temperature is 0°. After opening, place plastic wrap directly on the surface of the ice cream or sherbet to prevent ice crystals from forming.

Add a flavorful dimension to vanilla ice cream by topping a scoop with refreshing Lemon Curd or Praline-Pecan Sauce. These sauces will keep in the refrigerator for a couple of weeks and can be put in jars and tied with ribbons for attractive gifts.

Serve Favorite Apple Pie (page 155) with Old-Fashioned Vanilla Ice Cream (page 160). These two all-American desserts are guaranteed to please the entire family.

Carrot-Pineapple Cake

2 cups all-purpose flour
2½ teaspoons baking powder
¾ teaspoon salt
2 teaspoons ground cinnamon
2 cups sugar
2 cups shredded carrot
1¼ cups vegetable oil
4 eggs, beaten
1 (8¼-ounce) can crushed
    pineapple, undrained
¾ cup chopped pecans
Cream Cheese Frosting

Cream Cheese Frosting

½ cup butter or margarine,
    softened
1 (8-ounce) package cream
    cheese, softened
1 (16-ounce) package powdered
    sugar, sifted
1 teaspoon vanilla extract

Combine first 5 ingredients in a large bowl; stir in carrot, oil, eggs, pineapple, and pecans, mixing well.

Pour batter into a greased and floured 13- x 9- x 2-inch baking pan. Bake 325° for 45 to 55 minutes or until a wooden pick inserted in center comes out clean. Cool completely on a wire rack.

TO STORE: Cover tightly, and freeze up to 2 weeks.

TO SERVE: Thaw at room temperature. Spread Cream Cheese Frosting over cake. Yield: 15 servings.

Cream butter and cream cheese. Gradually add powdered sugar; beat until mixture is light and fluffy. Stir in vanilla. Yield: 3 cups.

Refreshing Lemon Cheesecake

1½ cups graham cracker crumbs
2 tablespoons sugar
¼ cup plus 2 tablespoons butter
    or margarine, melted
3 (8-ounce) packages cream
    cheese, softened
¾ cup sugar
3 eggs
1 tablespoon grated lemon rind
¼ cup fresh lemon juice
1 teaspoon vanilla extract
2 cups sour cream
3 tablespoons sugar
Garnishes: lemon roses, lemon
    rind curls, and fresh mint
    sprig

Combine first 3 ingredients, stirring well. Firmly press mixture evenly on bottom and 1 inch up sides of a 9-inch springform pan. Bake at 350° for 5 minutes. Cool.

Beat cream cheese at high speed of an electric mixer until light and fluffy; gradually add ¾ cup sugar, beating well. Add eggs, one at a time, beating well after each addition. Stir in grated lemon rind, lemon juice, and vanilla. Pour mixture into prepared crust. Bake at 375° for 40 to 45 minutes or until set.

Combine sour cream and 3 tablespoons sugar; stir well. Spread mixture evenly over cheesecake. Bake at 500° for 5 minutes. Cool completely on a wire rack.

TO STORE: Cover and refrigerate at least 8 hours and up to 2 days. Cover tightly, and freeze up to 2 weeks.

TO SERVE: Thaw in refrigerator. Carefully remove sides of springform pan. Garnish, if desired. Yield: one 9-inch cheesecake.

Serve Refreshing Lemon Cheesecake for a delicious ending to an outdoor summer dinner. Lemon roses and lemon rind curls are the perfect garnish.

Vanilla Chip Cookies

½ cup butter or margarine, softened
¼ cup plus 2 tablespoons sugar
¼ cup plus 2 tablespoons firmly packed brown sugar
1 egg
¾ teaspoon vanilla extract
1¼ cups all-purpose flour
½ teaspoon baking soda
½ teaspoon salt
1 cup vanilla milk chips
½ cup chopped pecans

Cream butter in a large mixing bowl; gradually add sugars, beating at medium speed of an electric mixer. Add egg and vanilla, mixing well.

Combine flour, soda, and salt; gradually add to creamed mixture, mixing well. Stir in chips and pecans. Shape dough into a 15-inch roll.

TO STORE: Wrap roll in wax paper, and refrigerate at least 2 hours and up to 24 hours. To freeze, wrap roll in wax paper, and then in heavy-duty aluminum foil. Freeze up to 1 month.

TO SERVE: Unwrap roll, and cut into ½-inch slices; place cut side down on ungreased baking sheets. Bake at 350° for 8 to 10 minutes or until cookies are light golden brown. Cool slightly; remove to wire racks to cool completely. Yield: about 2½ dozen.

Date-Nut Dessert Cheese

⅔ cup walnuts, lightly toasted
⅔ cup chopped dates
8 ounces sharp Cheddar cheese, cut into 1-inch pieces
1 (8-ounce) package cream cheese, softened and cut into 1-inch pieces
3 to 4 tablespoons dark rum

Position knife blade in food processor bowl. Add walnuts; top with cover, and pulse 6 times or until coarsely chopped. Remove walnuts, and set aside.

Position knife blade in processor bowl; add dates, and top with cover. Process 1 minute or until finely chopped. Add Cheddar cheese, cream cheese, and rum. Process 2 minutes, scraping sides of processor bowl occasionally.

Line a 2-cup mold with plastic wrap, extending plastic wrap over edges of mold. Spoon cheese mixture into mold, pressing firmly with the back of a spoon. Bring ends of plastic wrap over cheese mixture.

TO STORE: Cover and refrigerate at least 4 hours and up to 4 days.

TO SERVE: Unmold cheese, and remove plastic wrap. Press reserved walnuts on top and sides of cheese. Serve with gingersnaps and apple and pear slices. Yield: 2 cups.

Offer Date-Nut Dessert Cheese with gingersnaps and sliced apples and pears. Serve this whenever you want a not-too-sweet dessert.

Chocolate-Orange Crème in Meringue Shells ____

3 egg whites
¼ teaspoon cream of tartar
½ teaspoon vanilla extract
Dash of salt
½ cup sugar
Chocolate-Orange Crème
Garnishes: kumquat slices or
   small orange wedges

Beat egg whites (at room temperature) and cream of tartar at high speed of an electric mixer just until foamy; add vanilla and salt, beating until soft peaks form. Gradually add sugar, 1 tablespoon at a time, beating until stiff peaks form and sugar dissolves (2 to 4 minutes).

Line a baking sheet with heavy brown paper. Draw eight 3-inch circles on paper. Pipe meringue onto circles on brown paper, building up sides to form a shell. Bake at 200° for 1 hour and 15 minutes to 1 hour and 30 minutes. Turn oven off. Cool completely in oven at least 2 hours or overnight with oven door closed.

TO STORE: Place meringue shells in an airtight container, and store in a cool, dry place up to 2 weeks.

TO SERVE: Fill shells with Chocolate-Orange Crème. Garnish, if desired. Yield: 8 servings.

Chocolate-Orange Crème

¼ cup plus 2 tablespoons sugar
⅓ cup water
1 (6-ounce) package semisweet
   chocolate morsels
3 eggs, separated
2 teaspoons grated orange rind
½ teaspoon vanilla extract
½ teaspoon orange extract
¼ teaspoon cream of tartar
3 tablespoons sugar
¾ cup whipping cream,
   whipped

Combine ¼ cup plus 2 tablespoons sugar and water in a medium saucepan. Cook over medium-low heat until sugar dissolves, stirring constantly. Reduce heat to low; add chocolate, and cook until chocolate melts, stirring occasionally. Remove from heat.

Beat egg yolks in a medium bowl until thick and lemon colored. Gradually stir about one-fourth of chocolate mixture into yolks; add to remaining chocolate mixture, stirring constantly. Place mixture over medium heat, and bring to a boil. Cook 2 minutes, stirring constantly. Remove from heat, and stir in orange rind and flavorings. Let cool, stirring occasionally.

Beat egg whites (at room temperature) and cream of tartar at high speed of an electric mixer just until foamy. Gradually add 3 tablespoons sugar, 1 tablespoon at a time, beating until stiff peaks form and sugar dissolves. Fold beaten egg whites and whipped cream into chocolate mixture.

TO STORE: Cover and refrigerate up to 24 hours. Yield: 4 cups.

Chocolate-Orange Crème in Meringue Shells is a showy dessert that is surprisingly easy to prepare.

Favorite Apple Pie

Pastry for double-crust 9-inch
   pie
6½ cups peeled, sliced cooking
   apple
1 tablespoon lemon juice
¼ cup golden raisins
½ cup sugar
½ cup firmly packed brown
   sugar
¼ cup all-purpose flour
1 teaspoon grated lemon rind
1 teaspoon ground cinnamon
¼ teaspoon ground nutmeg
¼ teaspoon ground cloves
3 tablespoons butter or
   margarine

Roll half of pastry to ⅛-inch thickness on a lightly floured surface. Place in a 9-inch pieplate; trim off excess pastry along edges. Set aside.

Combine apple, lemon juice, and raisins in a large bowl, tossing to coat; set aside. Combine ½ cup sugar and next 6 ingredients in a small bowl. Spread half of sugar mixture over bottom of pastry shell. Spoon apple mixture over sugar mixture; sprinkle with remaining sugar mixture. Dot with butter.

Roll remaining pastry to ⅛-inch thickness, and place over filling. Trim off excess pastry along edges. Fold edges under and flute. Make decorative cutouts for top crust using excess pastry, if desired. Cut several slits in top crust to allow steam to escape.

TO STORE: Carefully wrap pie in heavy-duty aluminum foil. Label and freeze up to 1 month.

TO SERVE: Place frozen pie on a baking sheet. Bake, uncovered, at 475° for 15 minutes. Shield edge of pie with aluminum foil to prevent overbrowning. Reduce heat to 375°, and bake 1 hour or until golden brown. Cool before serving. Yield: one 9-inch pie.

Lemon-Orange Tarts

1½ cups all-purpose flour
2 tablespoons sugar
½ teaspoon baking powder
½ teaspoon salt
¼ cup butter or margarine,
   softened
¼ cup shortening
3 tablespoons milk
Lemon-Orange Filling
Garnishes: whipped cream,
   orange zest strips, and fresh
   mint sprigs

Combine first 4 ingredients in a large bowl; cut in butter and shortening with a pastry blender until mixture resembles coarse meal. Sprinkle milk (1 tablespoon at a time) over surface of mixture; stir with a fork until dry ingredients are moistened. Shape dough into a ball; chill 2 hours.

Divide dough into 8 equal portions. Roll each portion to ⅛-inch thickness on a lightly floured surface. Fit pastry into eight 4-inch tart pans. Prick bottom and sides of crust generously with a fork.

Bake at 450° for 8 to 10 minutes or until edges of pastry are lightly browned. Cool.

TO STORE: Refrigerate tart shells in a tightly covered container up to 24 hours. Freeze shells in a labeled airtight container up to 1 month.

TO SERVE: Thaw at room temperature. Spoon Lemon-Orange Filling into tart shells. Garnish, if desired. Yield: eight 4-inch tarts.

Lemon-Orange Filling

2 cups sugar
1 cup butter or margarine
1 tablespoon grated lemon rind
1 tablespoon grated orange rind
⅓ cup fresh lemon juice
⅓ cup fresh orange juice
6 egg yolks, beaten

Combine first 6 ingredients in top of a double boiler. Bring water to a boil. Reduce heat to low; cook over simmering water, stirring constantly, until butter melts. Gradually stir about one-fourth of hot mixture into egg yolks; add to remaining hot mixture, stirring constantly. Cook over simmering water, stirring constantly, until mixture thickens and coats a metal spoon (15 to 20 minutes). Remove from heat; cool.

TO STORE: Refrigerate filling in a tightly covered container up to 3 days. Yield: 3 cups.

For your next party, serve individual Lemon-Orange Tarts. They look pretty garnished with whipped cream, orange zest, and fresh mint sprigs.

Coffee-Almond Tortoni

1 cup whipping cream
½ cup sugar, divided
1 teaspoon vanilla extract
¼ teaspoon almond extract
2 egg whites
¼ cup finely chopped almonds, toasted and divided
¼ cup flaked coconut, toasted and divided
1 teaspoon instant coffee granules

Combine whipping cream, ¼ cup sugar, and flavorings in a medium mixing bowl; beat at high speed of an electric mixer until soft peaks form.

Beat egg whites (at room temperature) at high speed of an electric mixer just until foamy. Gradually add remaining ¼ cup sugar, 1 tablespoon at a time, beating until soft peaks form. Fold in whipped cream mixture, 2 tablespoons almonds, and 2 tablespoons coconut; spoon half of mixture into 8 muffin cups lined with foil liners.

Stir coffee granules into remaining half of tortoni mixture; spoon over whipped cream mixture in muffin cups. Sprinkle with remaining 2 tablespoons almonds and 2 tablespoons coconut.

TO STORE: Cover tightly, and freeze 8 hours. Remove frozen tortoni from muffin pans, and place in a zip-top heavy-duty plastic bag. Freeze up to 1 month.

TO SERVE: Remove from freezer 15 minutes before serving. Yield: 8 servings.

Creamy Lemon Freeze in Lemon Shells

1 cup milk
1 cup whipping cream
1 cup sugar
3 tablespoons grated lemon rind
⅓ cup fresh lemon juice
Scalloped lemon shells (optional)
Garnish: fresh mint sprigs

Combine milk, whipping cream, and sugar in a medium bowl; stir until sugar dissolves. Cover and freeze 2 hours. Add rind and juice; beat at medium speed of an electric mixer 3 to 5 minutes or until thickened.

TO STORE: Cover tightly, and freeze at least 24 hours and up to 2 weeks.

TO SERVE: Scoop Creamy Lemon Freeze into scalloped lemon shells, if desired, or dessert dishes. Garnish, if desired. Serve immediately. Yield: about 4 cups.

Coffee, almonds, and coconut are combined in Coffee-Almond Tortoni for a dessert that will melt in your mouth.

Layered Ice Cream Dessert

¾ cup chocolate wafer crumbs,
   divided
1 cup butter or margarine
2 (1-ounce) squares
   unsweetened chocolate
2 cups sifted powdered sugar
3 eggs, separated
1 cup coarsely chopped pecans
1 quart vanilla ice cream,
   softened
Garnish: strawberry fans

Sprinkle ½ cup chocolate crumbs evenly in bottom of a 13- x 9- x 2-inch baking pan. Set aside.

Combine butter and chocolate in a large saucepan; cook over low heat until butter melts, stirring occasionally. Remove from heat; add powdered sugar, and beat at medium speed of an electric mixer 2 minutes. Add egg yolks, beating until smooth.

Beat egg whites (at room temperature) until stiff peaks form; fold into chocolate mixture. Carefully pour chocolate mixture over crumbs in pan, and sprinkle with pecans. Cover and freeze 4 hours or until firm.

Spread ice cream evenly over pecan layer; sprinkle with remaining ¼ cup chocolate crumbs.

TO STORE: Cover tightly; freeze until dessert is firm and up to 2 weeks.

TO SERVE: Cut into squares, and garnish, if desired. Serve immediately. Yield: 15 servings.

Blueberry and Ice Cream Crêpes

1½ cups all-purpose flour
1 tablespoon sugar
¼ teaspoon salt
2 cups milk
1 teaspoon vanilla extract
3 eggs
2 tablespoons butter or
   margarine, melted
Vegetable oil
2 cups fresh or frozen
   blueberries, thawed
⅓ cup sugar
1 quart vanilla ice cream
1½ cups whipping cream,
   whipped
Additional fresh blueberries
Garnish: edible flowers

Any occasion will be special when your menu includes elegant Blueberry and Ice Cream Crêpes.

Combine first 3 ingredients; stir well. Add milk and vanilla; beat at medium speed of an electric mixer until smooth. Add eggs, and beat well; stir in butter. Refrigerate at least 1 hour. (This allows flour particles to swell and soften so that crepes will be light in texture.)

Brush the bottom of a 6-inch crêpe pan or heavy skillet with oil; place over medium heat just until hot, not smoking. Pour 2 tablespoons batter into pan; quickly tilt pan in all directions so that batter covers pan in a thin film. Cook about 1 minute or until lightly browned.

Lift edge of crêpe to test for doneness. Crêpe is ready for flipping when it can be shaken loose from pan. Flip crêpe, and cook about 30 seconds on other side. (This side is usually spotty brown and is the side on which the filling is placed.)

Place crêpe on a towel to cool. Repeat until all batter is used. Stack crêpes between layers of wax paper to prevent sticking.

TO STORE: Freeze crêpes in a labeled airtight container up to 2 weeks.

TO SERVE: Thaw crêpes at room temperature. Combine blueberries and ⅓ cup sugar; stir gently, and set aside. Fill each crêpe with about ¼ cup ice cream. Roll up, and place seam side up on a dessert plate. Top each crêpe with blueberry mixture, whipped cream, and additional fresh blueberries. Garnish, if desired. Serve immediately. Yield: 14 servings.

Coming Home to Supper

*F*ew thoughts are as comforting on busy days as knowing that supper is ready to heat and serve when you get home. You can forget weariness while visualizing a warming winter meal of Savory Meat Loaf with Old-Fashioned Macaroni and Cheese, or the summer refreshment of Grilled Swordfish with Lemon-Dill Butter and crisp Tangy Refrigerator Slaw.

Each of the menus in this chapter includes three do-ahead recipes. The recipes are as simple as possible, with most of the steps spread over a variety of time spans to let you choose the one that fits your schedule.

With a few minor changes, any one of these suppers can become a company dinner. The Summer Supper for Two menu suggests watermelon for dessert; you could enhance the meal by changing to Watermelon Sorbet from the Grilled Kabob Supper menu. Similarly, the Spinach Salad with Blue Cheese Dressing from the Neighborly Dinner would make the Put on a Pot of Chili menu perfect for a party, and something as simple as vanilla ice cream with Rich Caramel Sauce from the Mexican Fiesta menu would add a festive touch.

For added convenience, make an extra batch of meatballs or chili when ground beef is on sale. One meat loaf can be baked and frozen in slices for quick sandwich fixings.

When time is really at a premium, you can substitute a similar commercial item for a recipe in the menu. These may include salad ingredients from the supermarket salad bar, deli cole slaw, bakery bread, or a commercial dessert.

Three Pepper Pizza and Romaine Salad Italiano are ready in a flash to serve after a busy day. Menu begins on page 186.

Mexican Fiesta

Corn Salad Caliente

Burrito Supreme Casserole

Spanish rice

Vanilla ice cream with Rich Caramel Sauce

Serves 4

Bring the lively flavors and colors of Mexico to life with a menu guaranteed to rouse an olé from family members and friends.

Warm the casserole just before serving, and then add the finishing touch with a sprinkling of fresh lettuce, tomato, and avocado. A colorful marinated corn salad and commercial Spanish rice round out the menu.

Vanilla ice cream with a rich caramel sauce balances the spicy dishes from dinner, making it the perfect ending for this fiesta of flavor.

Corn Salad Caliente

2 (10-ounce) packages frozen corn, cooked and drained
1 (15½-ounce) can kidney beans, drained
¾ cup commercial oil and vinegar salad dressing
1 small purple onion, thinly sliced
1 small green pepper, cut into strips
½ cup (2 ounces) Monterey Jack cheese with jalapeño pepper, diced
½ cup sliced celery
½ cup sliced ripe olives
1 (2-ounce) jar diced pimiento, undrained
½ teaspoon salt
¼ teaspoon ground cumin
⅛ teaspoon ground red pepper

Combine all ingredients in a large bowl; toss gently.

TO STORE: Cover and refrigerate up to 24 hours.

TO SERVE: Serve with a slotted spoon. Yield: 4 to 6 servings.

Burrito Supreme Casserole

8 (8-inch) flour tortillas
1½ cups tomato juice
1 (1¼-ounce) envelope taco
   seasoning mix
1 tablespoon vegetable oil
½ pound ground beef
1 (16-ounce) can refried beans
3 cups (12 ounces) shredded
   Cheddar cheese, divided
1 small avocado
1 tablespoon lemon juice
1½ cups shredded lettuce
1 cup chopped tomato

Wrap tortillas securely in aluminum foil; bake at 350° for 15 minutes or until thoroughly heated.

Combine tomato juice, seasoning mix, and oil; stir well, and set aside.

Cook ground beef in a large skillet until browned, stirring to crumble; drain. Stir in beans and ½ cup tomato juice mixture. Bring to a boil; cover, reduce heat, and simmer 5 minutes or until mixture is thoroughly heated, stirring occasionally. Remove from heat.

Place ¼ cup beef mixture and 2½ tablespoons cheese down center of each tortilla. Roll up tortillas, and place seam side down in a lightly greased 13- x 9- x 2-inch baking dish.

TO STORE: Cover casserole, and refrigerate 8 hours. Refrigerate remaining tomato juice mixture in a tightly covered container.

TO SERVE: Pour remaining tomato juice mixture over casserole. Cover and bake, at 350° for 30 to 35 minutes. Uncover and sprinkle with remaining cheese; bake an additional 5 minutes or until cheese melts.

Peel and cube avocado; toss with lemon juice. Sprinkle avocado, lettuce, and tomato over casserole. Serve immediately. Yield: 4 servings.

Rich Caramel Sauce

½ cup plus 1 tablespoon
   sweetened condensed milk
¼ cup plus 2 tablespoons light
   corn syrup
¼ cup sugar
3 tablespoons brown sugar
3 tablespoons whipping cream
2 tablespoons butter or
   margarine
½ teaspoon vanilla extract
Vanilla ice cream

Combine first 4 ingredients in a heavy saucepan; stir well. Cook over medium heat, stirring constantly, until mixture reaches 220° on a candy thermometer. Remove from heat; stir in whipping cream, butter, and vanilla. Cool completely.

TO STORE: Refrigerate in a tightly covered container up to 4 days.

TO SERVE: Reheat in a saucepan over low heat, stirring occasionally, or microwave at HIGH for 2 to 4 minutes or until thoroughly heated, stirring occasionally. Serve warm over ice cream. Yield: 1½ cups.

Stir-Fry Delight

Chicken and Broccoli Stir-Fry

Sweet-and-Sour Slaw

Chinese fried noodles or rice

Orange-Coconut Crème

Serves 4

You don't need a wok to enjoy a tasty stir-fry. A large, heavy skillet works just as well.

Serve Chicken and Broccoli Stir-Fry over Chinese fried noodles or rice for a flavorful entrée. There's no time to prepare ingredients once you begin to stir-fry, so be sure to chop, measure, and assemble the ingredients before heating the skillet or wok.

A tangy slaw and a sweet orange dessert made the night before are easy additions to this quick supper.

Chicken and Broccoli Stir-Fry

¼ cup soy sauce
¼ cup dry sherry
2 tablespoons rice wine vinegar
2 tablespoons hoisin sauce
1 tablespoon brown sugar
½ cup chopped green onions
4 chicken breast halves, skinned and boned
2 tablespoons vegetable oil
3 cups broccoli flowerets
1 cup sliced fresh mushrooms
1 tablespoon cornstarch
¼ cup water
Chinese fried noodles or hot cooked rice

Combine first 6 ingredients in a medium bowl, stirring well; set aside. Cut chicken into 2-inch strips; add chicken to marinade, tossing to coat.

TO STORE: Refrigerate in a tightly covered container up to 24 hours.

TO SERVE: Pour oil around top of a preheated wok or skillet, coating sides; heat at medium high (325°) for 1 minute. Remove chicken from marinade. Place marinade in a small saucepan; bring to a boil, and cook 5 minutes. Set aside.

Add chicken to wok; stir-fry 2 to 3 minutes. Remove chicken, and set aside. Add broccoli to wok, and stir-fry 2 minutes. Add mushrooms; stir-fry 2 minutes or until vegetables are crisp-tender. Return chicken to wok; add marinade, stirring well. Combine cornstarch and water; add to wok. Cook, stirring constantly, until thickened. Serve chicken mixture over Chinese fried noodles or hot cooked rice. Yield: 4 servings.

Chicken and Broccoli Stir-Fry is a quick and colorful main dish. Serve it over a bed of Chinese fried noodles for a change from basic rice.

Chic

2 small
2 tablesp
 margar
½ teaspo
½ teaspo
½ teaspo
½ teaspo
¼ teaspo
¼ teaspo
¼ teaspo
¼ teaspo
¼ teaspo
¾ cup ca
 broth
Juice of
3 cups c

Nut

2 cups w
2 tablesp
 margar
½ teaspo
1 cup lo
1 cup fir
 toasted
½ cup fr
 thawed

Sweet-and-Sour Slaw

2 cups shredded cabbage
2 cups shredded red cabbage
¾ cup shredded carrot
½ cup cider vinegar
¼ cup vegetable oil
3 tablespoons sugar
½ teaspoon ground ginger
¼ teaspoon ground red pepper

Combine cabbage and carrot in a large bowl; set aside. Combine vinegar and oil in a small saucepan; stir in sugar, ginger, and red pepper. Cook over low heat, stirring constantly, until sugar dissolves. Immediately pour hot vinegar mixture over vegetables; toss well.

TO STORE: Refrigerate in a tightly covered container at least 8 hours and up to 1 week. Yield: 4 servings.

Orange-Coconut Crème

1 (3-ounce) package
 orange-flavored gelatin
1 cup boiling water
Grated rind of 1 orange
¾ cup orange juice
2 teaspoons lemon juice
1 cup whipping cream
¼ cup sugar
¼ cup flaked coconut
Garnishes: whipped cream and
 mandarin orange slices

Dissolve gelatin in boiling water. Stir in orange rind, orange juice, and lemon juice. Chill until mixture is the consistency of unbeaten egg white.

Beat 1 cup whipping cream at high speed of an electric mixer until foamy; gradually add sugar, beating until stiff peaks form. Fold sweetened whipped cream and coconut into gelatin mixture; spoon into 4 stemmed glasses.

TO STORE: Cover and refrigerate up to 24 hours.

TO SERVE: Garnish, if desired. Yield: 4 servings.

Easy Sunday Supper

Dijon Chicken

Crisp Carrot Marinade

Baked Cinnamon Apples

Chocolate ice cream with fudge sauce

Serves 4

Sunday evening is a time for relaxing before another busy week begins.

Relaxing is easy when you serve a supper on Sunday that was prepared on Saturday. All you have to do to complete the evening meal is bake the chicken and apples, and serve the marinated carrots on the side.

Something as simple as ice cream topped with a commercial fudge sauce is the perfect ending to this no-fuss meal.

A

½
2
½
5

⅓
1
1
½
½

½
¼

½

Dijon Chicken

4 chicken breast halves, skinned
　and boned
¼ cup butter or margarine,
　softened
¼ cup chopped green onions
2 tablespoons Dijon mustard
2 tablespoons lemon juice
2 tablespoons brandy
½ teaspoon salt
¼ teaspoon pepper

Place each piece of chicken between 2 sheets of heavy-duty plastic wrap; flatten to ¼-inch thickness, using a meat mallet or rolling pin. Place chicken in a lightly greased 11- x 7- x 1½-inch baking dish.

Combine butter and remaining ingredients; stir well. Spread butter mixture evenly over chicken.

TO STORE: Cover and refrigerate up to 24 hours.

TO SERVE: Bake, uncovered, at 350° for 30 to 35 minutes or until tender. Yield: 4 servings.

174

This relaxing Sunday supper includes Dijon Chicken, Baked Cinnamon Apples, and Crisp Carrot Marinade, a simple but attractive combination.

Crisp Carrot Marinade

1 pound carrots, scraped and
   thinly sliced
⅓ cup chopped onion
⅓ cup chopped green pepper
⅓ cup vinegar
⅓ cup sugar
3 tablespoons vegetable oil
1 teaspoon Worcestershire sauce
¼ teaspoon prepared mustard
Curly leaf lettuce

Cook carrot in boiling water to cover 5 minutes or until crisp-tender; drain.

Combine carrot, onion, and green pepper in a medium bowl. Combine vinegar and next 4 ingredients in a jar. Cover tightly, and shake vigorously. Pour dressing over vegetables; toss well.

TO STORE: Refrigerate in a tightly covered container up to 2 days.

TO SERVE: Serve on lettuce leaves, using a slotted spoon. Yield: 4 servings.

Baked Cinnamon Apples

4 large Rome apples
¼ cup firmly packed brown
   sugar
2 teaspoons ground cinnamon
½ cup apple juice
2 tablespoons butter or
   margarine, melted

Core apples to within ½ inch from bottom. Place apples in an 8-inch square baking dish. Combine brown sugar and cinnamon; spoon about 1 tablespoon sugar mixture into center of each apple.

TO STORE: Cover and refrigerate up to 24 hours.

TO SERVE: Pour apple juice into baking dish. Brush apples with melted butter. Cover and bake at 400° for 30 to 35 minutes. Yield: 4 servings.

Summer Supper for Two

Grilled Swordfish with Lemon-Dill Butter

Grilled Zucchini and Squash

Tangy Refrigerator Slaw

French bread

Watermelon

Serves 2

You can keep the kitchen cool when you serve a summer patio supper from the grill. The swordfish and squash serve two, but the recipes can be doubled or tripled for a crowd.

The flavored butter for the fish is ready in the freezer, and any remaining slaw will keep nicely in the refrigerator for up to a week.

A refreshing dessert is made simply by serving a slice of ice cold watermelon; it's easy on the waistline and easy on the cook!

Grilled Swordfish with Lemon-Dill Butter

2 tablespoons butter or margarine, softened
1 teaspoon grated lemon rind
1 teaspoon lemon juice
1½ tablespoons minced fresh dillweed
1 small clove garlic, minced
2 (¾-inch-thick) swordfish steaks (about ¾ pound)

Combine first 5 ingredients; stir well. Freeze mixture until slightly firm; shape into a cube.

TO STORE: Cover and refrigerate up to 1 week. Cover tightly, and freeze up to 1 month.

TO SERVE: Grill swordfish steaks over hot coals 5 to 7 minutes on each side or until fish flakes easily when tested with a fork. Soften butter slightly, and cut into 4 pats. Top each steak with 2 pats of butter. Serve immediately. Yield: 2 servings.

Baste Grilled Zucchini and Squash with a flavorful marinade while it cooks. Sweet red peppers add a splash of color.

Grilled Zucchini and Squash _____

1 medium-size yellow squash
1 medium zucchini
1 small sweet red pepper
½ cup vegetable oil
2 teaspoons grated lemon rind
1 teaspoon white wine vinegar
¼ cup fresh lemon juice
2 cloves garlic, minced
2 teaspoons dried whole basil
1 teaspoon dried whole oregano
1 teaspoon dried whole savory
1 teaspoon pepper

Wash vegetables thoroughly; cut into 1-inch pieces. Place vegetables in an 11- x 7- x 1½-inch baking dish.

Combine oil and remaining ingredients in a jar. Cover tightly, and shake vigorously; pour over vegetables.

TO STORE: Cover and refrigerate up to 24 hours.

TO SERVE: Remove vegetables from marinade. Alternate vegetables on four 6-inch skewers. Grill vegetables over hot coals 8 to 10 minutes or until tender, turning once and basting frequently with marinade. Yield: 2 servings.

Tangy Refrigerator Slaw _____

3 cups shredded cabbage
½ cup finely chopped green
   pepper
⅓ cup finely chopped onion
6 pimiento-stuffed olives, sliced
⅛ teaspoon salt
3 tablespoons vinegar
3 tablespoons vegetable oil
2 tablespoons sugar
¼ teaspoon celery seeds
⅛ teaspoon mustard seeds

Combine first 5 ingredients in a medium bowl; toss well, and set aside.

Combine vinegar, oil, sugar, celery seeds, and mustard seeds in a small saucepan; bring to a boil. Pour dressing mixture over vegetables; toss gently.

TO STORE: Refrigerate in a tightly covered container at least 8 hours and up to 1 week.

TO SERVE: Serve with a slotted spoon. Yield: 2 to 4 servings.

Ready for Entertaining

A good party starts in the imagination; picture a warm, lively scene, and then make it happen. Decide whom to invite, what day and time to have the party, and what to serve. Then set the stage with festive or elegant tableware, linens, and flowers. Do the planning in small steps over a period of time, leading up to "opening night." You'll find timing suggestions with each of the following menus. Study these suggestions; then adapt them to your own schedule.

The menus in this chapter highlight year-round occasions for entertaining. For springtime there is a Lunch for the Ladies and a Race-Day Brunch; for summer, a Cookout on the Patio and a Picnic in the Park; for winter, a Supper After the Theater and a Cocktail Buffet for Forty. Whichever menu you choose, remember that careful planning puts you in a better position to enjoy your own party.

To make your party go smoothly, imagine it happening, and write down the details that will need your attention. Start with the doorbell ringing. Where will guests put their coats? What beverages, alcoholic and non-alcoholic, will you offer? What appetizers will you offer? Will the food be placed in the living room, den, or out on the patio? Anticipating the answers to these "party production" questions goes hand-in-hand with do-ahead cooking to ensure starring roles for you and your food.

For a memorable cookout, include Two Bean and Cheese Salad, Grilled Corn on the Cob, Herbed Tomato Wedges, and Marinated Flank Steak. Menu begins on page 212.

Beef and Cucumber-Stuffed Pitas

2 (1-pound) flank steaks
1 medium cucumber, thinly
  sliced
1 cup chopped purple onion
¼ cup vegetable oil, divided
3 tablespoons red wine vinegar,
  divided
2 teaspoons Dijon mustard
1 teaspoon salt
½ teaspoon dried whole thyme
¼ teaspoon pepper
4 (6-inch) whole wheat pita
  bread rounds, halved
Curly leaf lettuce

Trim fat from steaks; score on both sides in 1½-inch squares. Place steaks on a greased rack in a roasting pan. Broil 4 inches from heat 4 to 5 minutes on each side or to desired degree of doneness. Slice steaks diagonally across grain into thin slices. Cut slices into thin strips.

Combine cucumber, onion, 2 tablespoons oil, and 1 tablespoon vinegar; stir well. Combine remaining 2 tablespoons oil and 2 tablespoons vinegar, meat, mustard, and next 3 ingredients; toss well.

TO STORE: Refrigerate both mixtures separately in tightly covered containers up to 24 hours.

TO SERVE: Drain cucumber mixture. Line pita halves with lettuce leaves. Divide meat mixture evenly among pita halves, and top with cucumber mixture. Yield: 8 sandwiches.

Cherry Tomatoes in Basil Vinaigrette

24 large cherry tomatoes, halved
¼ cup plus 2 tablespoons
  chopped fresh basil
¼ cup plus 2 tablespoons olive
  oil
3 tablespoons red wine vinegar
½ teaspoon salt
⅛ teaspoon freshly ground
  pepper

Place tomatoes in a large zip-top heavy-duty plastic bag; sprinkle with basil. Combine oil and remaining ingredients in a jar. Cover tightly, and shake vigorously; pour over tomatoes. Turn plastic bag to coat tomatoes.

TO STORE: Refrigerate up to 24 hours, turning bag occasionally.

TO SERVE: Serve with a slotted spoon. Yield: 8 servings.

Orange Brownies

½ cup butter or margarine
¾ cup sugar
2 tablespoons orange juice
1 (6-ounce) package semisweet
  chocolate morsels
½ teaspoon grated orange rind
½ teaspoon vanilla extract
½ teaspoon orange extract
2 eggs
¾ cup all-purpose flour
¼ teaspoon baking soda
¼ teaspoon salt
½ cup finely chopped walnuts

Combine butter, sugar, and orange juice in a medium saucepan; cook over medium heat, stirring frequently, until mixture comes to a boil. Remove from heat. Add chocolate morsels, orange rind, and flavorings, stirring until chocolate melts. Add eggs, one at a time, beating well after each addition. Combine flour, soda, and salt; stir flour mixture and walnuts into chocolate mixture.

Pour batter into a greased and floured 9-inch square pan. Bake at 325° for 30 minutes. Cool completely on a wire rack. Cut into squares. Yield: 9 servings.

Celebrate springtime with a picnic that includes Beef and Cucumber-Stuffed Pitas and Cherry Tomatoes in Basil Vinaigrette.

Race-Day Brunch

Apricot-Almond Fruit Dip

Assorted fresh fruit

Strawberry-Romaine Salad

Country Ham Links

Cheese and Asparagus Strata

Sweet Potato Biscuits

Orange marmalade   Butter

Sweepstakes Tassies

Mint juleps

Serves 12

One of the premier racing events of the year is the Kentucky Derby, held every year on the first Saturday in May. Parties abound, but none is more eagerly anticipated than a pre-race brunch.

A traditional Derby brunch includes country ham, asparagus, and strawberries. A wise choice of make-ahead dishes will free the hostess so that she can enjoy her guests and the races.

Apricot-Almond Fruit Dip

2 (8-ounce) cartons sour cream
¾ cup apricot preserves
1 teaspoon almond extract
Garnishes: edible flower and
   fresh mint sprig

Combine first 3 ingredients; stir well.

TO STORE: Refrigerate in a tightly covered container up to 24 hours.

TO SERVE: Garnish, if desired. Serve with fresh fruit. Yield: 2½ cups.

Before the races begin, treat guests to Apricot-Almond Fruit Dip, served with fresh fruit, and Strawberry-Romaine Salad.

The Pleasures of Afternoon Tea

Creamy Cucumber Rolls

Curried Chicken Salad Puffs

Miniature Shrimp Quiches

Spiced Pineapple Scones

Butter   Jam

Fresh strawberries with powdered sugar

Favorite Tea Cakes

Tea

Cream   Lemon wedges   Sugar cubes

Serves 12

Guests will delight in the relaxed yet elegant atmosphere of an afternoon tea party. Most of the finger foods featured in this menu can be made in advance, and then frozen or refrigerated. So sit back, relax, and enjoy a spot of tea with special friends.

Creamy Cucumber Rolls

1 large cucumber, peeled and seeded
1 (8-ounce) package cream cheese, softened
⅓ cup minced green onions
1 tablespoon minced fresh parsley
1 tablespoon mayonnaise
¼ teaspoon salt
⅛ teaspoon ground white pepper
6 slices white bread
6 slices whole wheat bread

Shred and thoroughly drain cucumber; press between paper towels to remove excess moisture. Combine cucumber and next 6 ingredients in a medium bowl, and stir well.

TO STORE: Refrigerate cucumber mixture in a tightly covered container up to 2 days.

TO SERVE: Remove crust from bread. Flatten bread slices, using a rolling pin. Spread each slice with approximately 2 tablespoons cucumber filling, and roll up jelly-roll fashion. Cut each roll in half. Yield: 2 dozen.

Curried Chicken Salad Puffs

1 cup water
½ cup butter or margarine
1 cup all-purpose flour
¼ teaspoon salt
4 eggs
2 cups finely chopped cooked chicken
1 (8-ounce) can pineapple tidbits, drained
1 (8-ounce) can sliced water chestnuts, drained and finely chopped
½ cup finely chopped celery
½ cup mayonnaise
1½ teaspoons curry powder
1 teaspoon lemon juice
1 teaspoon soy sauce
¼ teaspoon salt

Combine water and butter in a saucepan; bring to a boil. Add flour and salt, all at once, stirring vigorously over low heat until mixture leaves sides of pan and forms a smooth ball. Cool 10 minutes. Add eggs, one at a time, beating well after each. (Mixture may separate as each egg is added; beat until smooth.) Drop dough by heaping teaspoonfuls 2 inches apart on ungreased baking sheets. Bake at 400° for 15 minutes. Reduce heat to 350°, bake 10 minutes or until puffed and golden. Cool on wire racks.

Combine chicken and remaining ingredients in a medium bowl; stir well.

TO STORE: Freeze cream puffs in a labeled airtight container up to 1 month. Refrigerate chicken salad mixture in a tightly covered container up to 24 hours.

TO SERVE: Thaw cream puffs at room temperature. Bake at 250° for 5 minutes. Cut tops off cream puffs; pull out and discard soft dough inside. Fill bottoms with 1 tablespoon chicken salad mixture; cover with tops. Yield: 5 dozen.

Dainty finger foods such as Curried Chicken Salad Puffs are ideal for an afternoon tea.

Miniature Shrimp Quiches

1 cup (4 ounces) shredded
  Swiss cheese
½ cup finely chopped cooked
  shrimp
2 tablespoons chopped fresh
  chives
½ teaspoon dried whole thyme
Pastry shells (recipe follows)
2 eggs, beaten
½ cup half-and-half
¼ teaspoon salt
¼ teaspoon ground nutmeg
¼ teaspoon pepper
Dash of hot sauce

Combine cheese, shrimp, chives, and thyme; spoon mixture evenly into pastry shells. Combine eggs and remaining ingredients, stirring well. Pour mixture into pastry shells, filling three-fourths full. Bake at 350° for 30 to 35 minutes or until set. Cool.

TO STORE: Refrigerate quiches in a tightly covered container up to 24 hours. Freeze quiches in a labeled airtight container up to 2 weeks.

TO SERVE: Thaw in refrigerator. Place quiches on baking sheets. Bake at 300° for 10 minutes or until hot. Yield: 3 dozen.

Pastry Shells

½ cup butter or margarine,
  softened
½ (8-ounce) package cream
  cheese, softened
1½ cups all-purpose flour
¼ teaspoon salt

Beat butter and cream cheese at medium speed of an electric mixer until well blended. Stir in flour and salt. Cover dough, and refrigerate 1 hour.

Shape chilled dough into 36 (1-inch) balls. Place in ungreased miniature (1¾-inch) muffin pans, shaping each ball into a shell. Yield: 3 dozen.

Spiced Pineapple Scones

2 cups all-purpose flour
2 teaspoons baking powder
½ teaspoon baking soda
¼ teaspoon salt
¼ cup sugar
½ teaspoon ground cinnamon
¼ teaspoon ground nutmeg
⅓ cup butter or margarine, softened
1 (8¼-ounce) can crushed pineapple, undrained
1 egg, beaten
¼ cup finely chopped almonds
1 tablespoon milk
1 tablespoon sugar

Combine first 7 ingredients in a medium bowl, stirring well; cut in butter with a pastry blender until mixture resembles coarse meal. Add pineapple, egg, and almonds, stirring just until dry ingredients are moistened (dough will be sticky). Turn dough out onto a floured surface, and knead lightly 4 or 5 times.

Pat dough to 2-inch thickness; cut with a floured 1½-inch cutter. Place on ungreased baking sheets. Brush tops lightly with milk, and sprinkle with 1 tablespoon sugar. Bake at 400° for 12 to 15 minutes or until golden brown. Cool.

TO STORE: Store scones at room temperature in a tightly covered container up to 24 hours. Freeze scones in a labeled airtight container up to 2 weeks.

TO SERVE: Thaw at room temperature. Place scones on baking sheets. Bake at 300° for 10 minutes or until hot. Yield: 2½ dozen.

Favorite Tea Cakes

½ cup butter or margarine, softened
1 cup sugar
1 egg
1 teaspoon vanilla extract
1 teaspoon grated lemon rind
2¾ cups all-purpose flour
½ teaspoon baking soda
½ teaspoon salt
¼ cup buttermilk
Sugar

Cream butter; gradually add 1 cup sugar, beating well at medium speed of an electric mixer. Add egg, vanilla, and lemon rind; beat well.

Combine flour, soda, and salt in a medium bowl; add to creamed mixture alternately with buttermilk, beginning and ending with flour mixture. Cover dough, and refrigerate at least 2 hours.

Roll dough to ¼-inch thickness on a lightly floured surface. Cut with a 2-inch cookie cutter, and place on lightly greased baking sheets; sprinkle with sugar. Bake at 375° for 6 to 8 minutes or until edges are lightly browned. Cool on wire racks.

TO STORE: Store cookies at room temperature in a tightly covered container up to 2 days. Freeze in a labeled airtight container up to 1 month.

TO SERVE: Thaw cookies at room temperature. Yield: 3½ dozen.

This menu wouldn't be complete without Favorite Tea Cakes. These light and crispy cakes are as good as the ones your grandmother used to make.

After-Work Dinner
for Company

Dill Dip

Assorted fresh vegetables

Spicy Baked Chicken Breasts

Wheat-Vegetable Pilaf

Marinated Asparagus

Cool Mocha Pie in Pecan Crust

Serves 6

Two-career couples can entertain friends during a busy week, but entertaining on a week night takes some planning. For a hassle-free weekday company dinner, choose do-ahead dishes that are ready, or ready to assemble, as soon as you walk into the kitchen. Bring the meal to a close with a coffee-laced chocolate pie in a pecan crust.

Dill Dip

1 cup mayonnaise
1 (8-ounce) carton sour cream
1½ tablespoons minced fresh parsley
1½ tablespoons grated onion
1 tablespoon dried whole dillweed
½ teaspoon seasoned salt
Garnish: fresh dillweed sprigs

Combine first 6 ingredients; stir well.

TO STORE: Refrigerate in a tightly covered container up to 1 week.

TO SERVE: Stir well. Garnish, if desired. Serve with assorted fresh vegetables. Yield: 2 cups.

Entertain on a week night by serving Spicy Baked Chicken Breasts, Marinated Asparagus, and Wheat-Vegetable Pilaf.

Spicy Baked Chicken Breasts

¼ cup orange juice
¼ cup pineapple juice
¼ cup lime juice
2 tablespoons vegetable oil
1 teaspoon grated lime rind
6 chicken breast halves, skinned
1 cup round buttery cracker crumbs
¼ teaspoon ground white pepper
¼ teaspoon ground ginger
⅛ teaspoon ground cumin
Garnish: fresh flat leaf parsley sprigs

Combine first 5 ingredients in a small bowl, stirring well. Place chicken in a shallow dish. Pour orange juice mixture over chicken.

TO STORE: Cover and refrigerate up to 24 hours.

TO SERVE: Combine cracker crumbs, pepper, ginger, and cumin in a plastic bag; shake to mix. Remove chicken from marinade; discard marinade. Place 2 pieces of chicken in bag, and shake to coat. Repeat procedure with remaining chicken. Place chicken in a lightly greased 13- x 9- x 2-inch baking dish. Cover and bake at 350° for 20 minutes; uncover and bake an additional 30 minutes or until tender. Garnish, if desired. Yield: 6 servings.

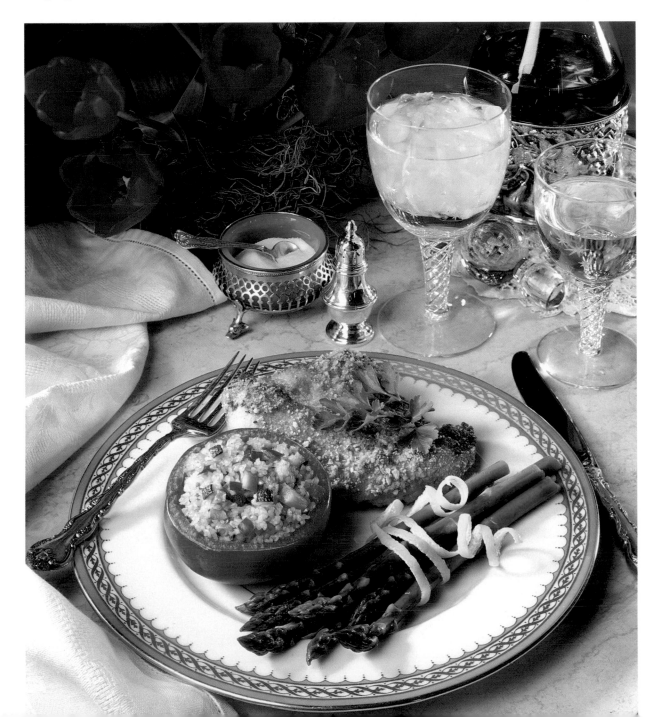

End the evening on an elegant note with Cool Mocha Pie in Pecan Crust. This luscious frozen dessert needs only a few minutes to thaw before serving.

Wheat-Vegetable Pilaf

1 small zucchini, thinly sliced
½ cup sliced green onions
½ cup chopped sweet red pepper
½ cup diced carrot
3 tablespoons butter or margarine, melted
1 cup bulgur wheat
2 cups chicken broth
½ teaspoon onion powder
¼ teaspoon salt
¼ teaspoon pepper
3 large tomatoes
¾ teaspoon salt

Sauté first 4 ingredients in butter in a large skillet 5 minutes or until vegetables are crisp-tender. Add bulgur wheat; sauté 5 minutes, stirring well. Stir in broth, onion powder, ¼ teaspoon salt, and pepper. Bring to a boil; cover, reduce heat, and simmer 20 minutes or until all liquid is absorbed.

Cut tomatoes in half. Scoop out pulp, leaving shells intact; reserve tomato pulp for other uses. Sprinkle inside of each tomato half with ⅛ teaspoon salt, and invert on paper towels to drain. Spoon bulgur mixture into tomato shells.

TO STORE: Refrigerate in a tightly covered container up to 24 hours.

TO SERVE: Place on ungreased baking sheets. Bake at 350° for 10 minutes. Yield: 6 servings.

Marinated Asparagus

1½ pounds fresh asparagus
½ cup sugar
½ cup cider vinegar
1½ tablespoons lemon juice
1 teaspoon salt
⅛ teaspoon seasoned pepper
Garnish: lemon rind curls

Snap off tough ends of asparagus. Remove scales with a knife or vegetable peeler, if desired. Cook asparagus, covered, in a small amount of boiling water 6 to 8 minutes or until crisp-tender; drain, reserving ½ cup liquid. Place asparagus in a large shallow container, and set aside.

Combine reserved liquid, sugar, and next 4 ingredients in a small saucepan; bring to a boil, stirring constantly. Pour mixture over asparagus.

TO STORE: Cover and refrigerate 8 hours.

TO SERVE: Arrange asparagus on a serving platter. Garnish, if desired. Yield: 6 servings.

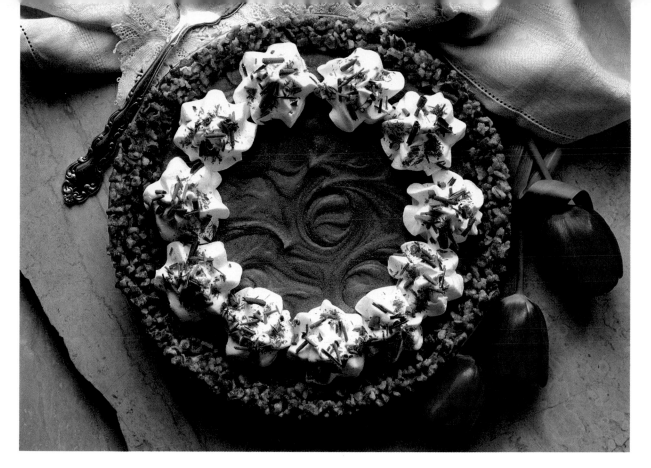

Cool Mocha Pie in Pecan Crust

6 (1-ounce) squares semisweet
  chocolate
½ teaspoon instant coffee
  granules
2 eggs, beaten
3 tablespoons Kahlúa or other
  coffee-flavored liqueur
¼ cup sifted powdered sugar
¾ cup whipping cream,
  whipped
1 teaspoon vanilla extract
Pecan Crust
¾ cup whipping cream
1 tablespoon Kahlúa or other
  coffee-flavored liqueur
Grated chocolate

Place chocolate squares and coffee granules in top of a double boiler; bring water to a boil. Reduce heat to low; cook until chocolate melts. Gradually stir about one-fourth of hot mixture into eggs; add to remaining hot mixture, stirring constantly. Gradually stir in 3 tablespoons Kahlúa and powdered sugar. Cook, stirring constantly, until mixture reaches 165° on a candy thermometer. Cool to room temperature.

Fold whipped cream into chocolate mixture. Stir in vanilla. Spoon mixture into Pecan Crust.

TO STORE: Cover tightly, and freeze at least 8 hours and up to 3 weeks.

TO SERVE: Place frozen pie in refrigerator 1 hour before serving. Beat ¾ cup whipping cream at high speed of an electric mixer until foamy; gradually add 1 tablespoon Kahlúa, beating until stiff peaks form. Pipe or dollop whipped cream around edge of pie. Sprinkle with grated chocolate. Yield: one 9-inch pie.

Pecan Crust

1¾ cups finely chopped pecans
⅓ cup firmly packed brown
  sugar
3 tablespoons butter or
  margarine, melted
2 teaspoons Kahlúa or other
  coffee-flavored liqueur

Combine all ingredients, stirring well. Firmly press mixture evenly over bottom and up sides of a 9-inch pieplate. Bake at 350° for 10 to 12 minutes. Press sides of crust with the back of a spoon to flatten. Cool. Yield: one 9-inch crust.

The Boss Comes to Dinner

Overnight Chicken Divan

Wild Rice Salad

Tangy Marinated Carrots

French bread

Chocolate Dream Dessert

Serves 8

On that important night when the boss comes to dinner even the calmest host or hostess can feel nervous.

When you serve an array of enticing do-ahead food, the last thing you will have to worry about is the menu. There's no reason to panic at the last minute because everything will be done except baking the chicken and heating the bread. Offer a glass of wine, and relax with your guests instead of worrying about last-minute preparations.

Overnight Chicken Divan

8 chicken breast halves
1 teaspoon salt
2 (10-ounce) packages frozen broccoli spears
1 (10½-ounce) can cream of chicken soup, undiluted
½ cup sour cream
½ cup mayonnaise
2 tablespoons dry sherry
1 teaspoon paprika
1 teaspoon prepared mustard
¼ teaspoon curry powder
⅓ cup grated Parmesan cheese
Paprika

Combine chicken and salt in a Dutch oven; add enough water to cover chicken. Bring to a boil; cover, reduce heat, and simmer 1 hour or until tender. Remove chicken, and cool slightly. (Reserve broth for other uses.) Bone chicken, and coarsely chop meat; set aside.

Cook broccoli according to package directions; drain well. Arrange broccoli in a lightly greased 13- x 9- x 2-inch baking dish. Combine soup and next 6 ingredients; spoon half of sauce over broccoli. Arrange chicken over sauce; top with remaining sauce.

TO STORE: Cover and refrigerate up to 24 hours.

TO SERVE: Bake, uncovered, at 350° for 30 to 35 minutes or until thoroughly heated. Sprinkle with cheese and paprika; bake an additional 5 minutes. Yield: 8 servings.

Wild Rice Salad

1 (6-ounce) package long-grain and wild rice mix
3 green onions, cut into ½-inch pieces
1 (8-ounce) can sliced water chestnuts, drained
½ cup chopped walnuts, toasted
⅓ cup mayonnaise
Dash of pepper
Raddichio leaves

Cook rice according to package directions; cool slightly. Combine rice and next 5 ingredients; stir well.

TO STORE: Refrigerate in a tightly covered container up to 8 hours.

TO SERVE: Serve on raddichio leaves. Yield: 8 servings.

Tangy Marinated Carrots

5 cups scraped and thinly sliced carrots
¼ cup olive oil
¼ cup white wine vinegar
1 teaspoon dried whole basil
¼ teaspoon finely chopped garlic
½ teaspoon salt
Dash of freshly ground pepper

Cook carrots in boiling water to cover about 7 minutes or until crisp-tender; drain. Combine carrots and remaining ingredients in a medium bowl; toss gently.

TO STORE: Refrigerate in a tightly covered container up to 24 hours.

TO SERVE: Toss gently before serving. Serve with a slotted spoon. Yield: 8 servings.

Chocolate Dream Dessert

2 dozen ladyfingers, split lengthwise
¼ cup Kahlúa or other coffee-flavored liqueur
12 (1-ounce) squares semisweet chocolate
2 (8-ounce) packages cream cheese, softened
½ cup sugar
3 eggs, separated
2 teaspoons vanilla extract
2 cups whipping cream, whipped
Garnishes: sweetened whipped cream, chocolate curls, and maraschino cherries

Brush cut side of ladyfingers with Kahlúa. Line bottom and sides of a 9-inch springform pan with ladyfingers, placing rounded sides of ladyfingers toward pan. Set prepared pan aside.

Place chocolate squares in top of a double boiler; bring water to a boil over medium heat. Reduce heat to low; cook until chocolate melts. Cool.

Beat cream cheese and sugar at high speed of an electric mixer until light and fluffy. Add egg yolks, one at a time, beating well after each addition. Add melted chocolate and vanilla, stirring until smooth.

Beat egg whites (at room temperature) at high speed of electric mixer until stiff peaks form. Fold egg whites and whipped cream into chocolate mixture; pour into prepared pan.

TO STORE: Cover and refrigerate at least 8 hours and up to 24 hours.

TO SERVE: Carefully remove sides from pan. Garnish, if desired. Yield: 8 servings.

Supper After the Theater

Royal Seafood Casserole

Colorful Squash Marinade

Pinwheel Wheat Rolls

Orange Crème Cups

Celebrity Champagne Cocktail

Serves 6

For a fitting encore to an evening at the theater, invite friends over for an elegant late-night supper. The stars of the menu can be prepared ahead and served 30 to 45 minutes after guests arrive.

Royal Seafood Casserole

6 cups water
1½ pounds unpeeled medium-size fresh shrimp
½ (7-ounce) package vermicelli or thin spaghetti
⅓ cup butter or margarine
⅓ cup all-purpose flour
⅔ cup chicken broth
⅔ cup whipping cream
¾ cup (3 ounces) shredded Swiss cheese
2½ tablespoons dry sherry
½ teaspoon salt
⅛ teaspoon ground white pepper
1 (4-ounce) jar diced pimiento, drained
2 tablespoons grated Parmesan cheese
2 tablespoons slivered almonds
Garnish: chopped fresh parsley

Bring water to a boil; add shrimp, and cook 3 to 5 minutes. Drain well; rinse shrimp with cold water. Peel and devein shrimp; set aside.

Cook vermicelli according to package directions; drain well, and set aside.

Melt butter in a heavy saucepan over low heat; add flour, stirring until smooth. Cook 1 minute, stirring constantly. Gradually add broth and cream; cook over medium heat, stirring constantly, until mixture is thickened and bubbly. Add Swiss cheese, sherry, salt, and pepper, stirring until cheese melts. Remove from heat; add shrimp, vermicelli, and pimiento, stirring gently.

Spoon mixture into a lightly greased 2-quart casserole. Sprinkle with Parmesan cheese and almonds.

TO STORE: Cover and refrigerate up to 24 hours.

TO SERVE: Bake, uncovered, at 350° for 20 minutes or until thoroughly heated. Broil 6 inches from heat 6 minutes or until lightly browned. Garnish, if desired. Yield: 6 servings.

Entertaining friends after the show is easy with rich Royal Seafood Casserole and Pinwheel Wheat Rolls.

Salmon Mousse

2 envelopes unflavored gelatin
½ cup cold water
1 (15½-ounce) can red salmon, drained
1 cup mayonnaise
2 tablespoons vinegar
2 tablespoons catsup
Dash of ground red pepper
Dash of pepper
15 pimiento-stuffed olives, sliced
2 hard-cooked eggs, chopped
2 tablespoons sweet pickle relish
1 cup whipping cream, whipped
Flowering cabbage
Garnishes: lemon slices and chopped fresh parsley

Sprinkle gelatin over cold water in a small saucepan; let stand 1 minute. Cook over low heat, stirring until gelatin dissolves. Remove from heat, and set aside.

Remove skin and bones from salmon, if desired; flake salmon with a fork. Combine salmon and next 5 ingredients; stir well. Add reserved gelatin mixture, olives, egg, and relish; stir well. Gently fold in whipped cream. Spoon mixture into a well-greased 5½-cup mold.

TO STORE: Cover and refrigerate up to 2 days.

TO SERVE: Unmold onto a serving plate lined with flowering cabbage. Garnish, if desired. Serve with assorted crackers. Yield: 5½ cups.

Marinated Mushrooms and Artichokes

2 pounds small fresh mushrooms
2 (14-ounce) cans artichoke hearts, drained and quartered
½ cup olive oil
¼ cup vegetable oil
½ cup white wine vinegar
½ cup lemon juice
3 cloves garlic, minced
1 tablespoon chopped fresh parsley
1 teaspoon salt
1 teaspoon crushed red pepper
1 teaspoon dried whole basil
1 teaspoon dried whole oregano
½ teaspoon dried whole thyme
Garnish: fresh basil sprig

Combine mushrooms and artichokes in a large bowl. Combine olive oil and next 10 ingredients; stir well. Pour marinade over mushrooms and artichokes, tossing gently to coat.

TO STORE: Refrigerate in a tightly covered container up to 3 days, stirring occasionally.

TO SERVE: Spoon mixture into a serving bowl, using a slotted spoon. Garnish, if desired. Yield: about 8½ cups.

Salmon Mousse and Marinated Mushrooms and Artichokes are eye-catching additions to your cocktail buffet table.

Fruit and Cheese Logs

2 (8-ounce) packages cream
  cheese, softened
½ cup finely chopped dried
  apricots
½ cup chopped dates
2 tablespoons Grand Marnier or
  other orange-flavored liqueur
2 teaspoons grated orange rind
1½ cups finely chopped
  hazelnuts, toasted

Combine first 5 ingredients; stir well. Divide mixture in half. Spoon each half of mixture onto a large piece of wax paper, and shape into an 8-inch log. Roll each log in hazelnuts; wrap in wax paper.

TO STORE: Refrigerate up to 2 days.

TO SERVE: Slice logs, and serve with assorted crackers. Yield: two 8-inch logs.

Double Cheese Wafers

¾ cup butter or margarine,
  softened
⅔ cup shredded Cheddar cheese
⅔ cup crumbled Roquefort
  cheese
2 cups all-purpose flour
2 teaspoons minced fresh chives
1 teaspoon minced fresh parsley
½ teaspoon Worcestershire
  sauce
¼ teaspoon ground red pepper
⅛ teaspoon garlic powder
1 cup sesame seeds, toasted

Cream butter; add cheeses, and beat at medium speed of an electric mixer until well blended. Add flour and next 5 ingredients; mix well. Shape dough into a ball; cover and refrigerate at least 2 hours.
  Shape dough into ¾-inch balls; roll in sesame seeds. Place on lightly greased baking sheets, and flatten to ¼-inch thickness with a fork, making a crisscross pattern. Bake at 350° for 12 to 14 minutes or until edges are golden brown. Cool on wire racks.

TO STORE: Refrigerate wafers in a tightly covered container up to 3 days. Freeze in a labeled airtight container up to 1 month.

TO SERVE: Thaw wafers at room temperature. Yield: about 7 dozen.

Rosy Herb Dip

2 cups sour cream
1 (3-ounce) package cream
  cheese, softened
3 tablespoons tomato paste
3 tablespoons finely chopped
  onion
2 tablespoons chopped fresh
  parsley
1 clove garlic, minced
1 teaspoon sugar
1 teaspoon dried whole basil
1 teaspoon dried whole dillweed
¼ teaspoon salt
¼ teaspoon ground white
  pepper

Combine all ingredients in a medium bowl; stir well.

TO STORE: Refrigerate dip in a tightly covered container up to 2 days.

TO SERVE: Spoon dip into a serving bowl. Serve with assorted crudités. Yield: about 2⅔ cups.

Serve Rosy Herb Dip with a large platter of colorful fresh vegetables.

Dairy Products (continued)

Egg yolks

TO FREEZE: For dessert recipes, add 1 teaspoon sugar to each yolk. For sauces and egg dishes, add ½ teaspoon salt to each yolk. Place in an airtight container; seal and label. *Storage time: up to 3 weeks.*

TO SERVE: Thaw in refrigerator.

Whipped cream

TO FREEZE: Drop spoonfuls of whipped cream onto an aluminum foil-lined baking sheet; place in freezer. When frozen, store in a rigid airtight container, separating layers with wax paper. Seal and label. *Storage time: up to 1 month.*

TO SERVE: Place frozen spoonfuls of whipped cream on dessert, and allow to thaw until serving time.

Main-Dish Casseroles

Meat casseroles with pasta, vegetables

TO FREEZE: Prepare dish as directed, undercooking slightly. Cool quickly. Cover with moisture/vapor-proof material, or place in an airtight container. Seal and label. *Storage time: up to 1 month.*

TO SERVE: Thaw in refrigerator. Bake as directed.

Meats

Beef, veal, lamb, pork, cooked

TO FREEZE: Large cuts of meat dry out the least. Cover sliced meats with gravy or sauces, if possible, to retain moisture. Wrap meat in moisture/vapor-proof material, or place in an airtight container. Seal and label. *Storage time: up to 3 months.*

TO SERVE: Thaw in refrigerator. Defrost time will depend on size and amount of meat.

Country ham

TO FREEZE: An unsliced ham will keep longer than sliced ham. Wrap meat in moisture/vapor-proof material, or place in an airtight container. Seal and label. *Storage time: up to 3 months.*

TO SERVE: Thaw in refrigerator. Defrost time will depend on size and amount of meat.

Meatballs, meat loaf, cooked

TO FREEZE: Freeze meatballs in sauce to retain moisture. Wrap cooled meat in moisture/vapor-proof material, or place in an airtight container. Seal and label. *Storage time: up to 1 month.*

TO SERVE: Thaw in refrigerator. Wrap meat loaf in aluminum foil, and bake at 325° for 40 minutes or until thoroughly heated. Cook meatballs and sauce in a saucepan over medium heat 10 minutes or until thoroughly heated.

Meat pies

TO FREEZE: Cook meat and vegetables; cool quickly. Place in dish(es), and top with pastry. Cut slits in crust to allow steam to escape. Wrap pie(s) in moisture/vapor-proof material, or place in an airtight container. Seal and label. *Storage time: up to 1 month.*

TO SERVE: Bake at 400° for 45 minutes or until crust is golden.

Pies

Fruit, unbaked

TO FREEZE: Toss fruit with ascorbic acid or lemon juice to prevent darkening. Wrap prepared pie in heavy-duty aluminum foil; label. *Storage time: up to 1 month.*

TO SERVE: Bake as directed, shielding edges of pie with aluminum foil as necessary to prevent browning.

Ice cream with crumb crust

TO FREEZE: Wrap prepared pie in moisture/vapor-proof material, or place pie in an airtight container. Seal and label. *Storage time: up to 1 week.*

TO SERVE: Thaw, uncovered, at room temperature 20 to 30 minutes or until easy to cut, but slightly frozen.

Pastry shells, baked

TO FREEZE: Place dish containing baked pastry shell in freezer. When frozen, remove and stack shells in a rigid covered container, or store, covered, in disposable foil pans. *Storage time: up to 1 month.*

TO SERVE: Thaw, uncovered, at room temperature. Fill and serve as directed.

Pastry shells, unbaked

TO FREEZE: Prepare pastry as directed, and place in pieplate. Wrap in moisture/vapor-proof material, or place in an airtight container. Seal and label. *Storage time: up to 2 months.*

TO SERVE: Thaw slightly, uncovered, at room temperature. Follow specific baking instructions for the type of pie being baked.

Poultry

Chicken, turkey, cooked

TO FREEZE: Remove stuffing from cooked poultry before freezing. Wrap poultry in moisture/vapor-proof material, or place in an airtight container. Seal and label. *Storage time: up to 3 months.*

TO SERVE: Thaw in refrigerator. Defrost time will depend on size and amount of poultry.

Sandwiches

Cheese, meat, peanut butter

TO FREEZE: Wrap sandwiches in moisture/vapor-proof material, or place sandwiches in an airtight container. Seal and label. *Storage time: up to 2 weeks.*

TO SERVE: Thaw before serving. Some meat and cheese sandwiches may need to be thawed in the refrigerator.

Soups and Stews

Vegetable soups and stews

TO FREEZE: Select vegetables that freeze well; omit potatoes. Place cooled soup or stew in a labeled airtight container. Seal and label. *Storage time: up to 1 month.*

TO SERVE: Thaw in refrigerator. Heat in a large pan over medium-high heat until thoroughly heated, stirring occasionally.

Recipe Index

Biscuits
  Angel Biscuits, 129
  Poppy Seed-Dill
    Biscuits, 126
  Sweet Potato Biscuits, 207
Blueberries
  Crisp, Blueberry-Apple, 159
  Ice Cream Crêpes, Blueberry
    and, 165
  Pancakes, Blueberry, 35
Bran Muffins, Fruited
  Refrigerator, 32
Breads. See also specific types.
  Herbed Bread Italiano, 126
  Nut Bread Sandwiches,
    Tropical, 54
  Pesto-Parmesan Toasts, 193
  Scones, Spiced Pineapple, 211
  Yeast
    Cottage Cheese-Dill
      Bread, 185
    Sesame Breadsticks, 197
Broccoli
  Divan, Overnight
    Chicken, 218
  Ham and Broccoli Bake,
    Brunch, 39
  Rice Combo, Broccoli-, 130
  Soup, Creamy Chicken and
    Broccoli, 46
  Stir-Fry, Chicken and
    Broccoli, 170
Bulgur
  Pilaf, Wheat-Vegetable, 216
Burrito Supreme Casserole, 169
Butter
  Chive Butter, 21
  Cinnamon-Honey Butter, 21
  Garlic Butter, 21
  Lemon-Dill Butter, Grilled
    Swordfish with, 182
  Nut Butter, 21
  Orange Butter, 21
  Strawberry-Orange Butter,
    Fresh, 20

Cabbage
  Slaws
    Refrigerator Slaw,
      Tangy, 183
    Sweet-and-Sour Slaw, 171
  Sweet-and-Sour Red
    Cabbage, 139
Cakes. See also Breads,
  Cookies.
  Carrot-Pineapple Cake, 149

Cheesecakes
  Lemon Cheesecake,
    Refreshing, 149
  Peaches and Cream
    Cheesecake, 150
Chocolate
  Basic Chocolate Cake, 146
  Raspberry-Almond
    Chocolate Cake, 146
  White Chocolate Party
    Cake, 147
Cupcakes, Chocolate Chip, 187
Pound Cake, Sour
  Cream-Streusel, 150
Caramel Sauce, Rich, 169
Carrots
  Cake, Carrot-Pineapple, 149
  Marinade, Crisp Carrot, 179
  Marinated Carrots,
    Tangy, 219
  Soup, Cool Carrot-
    Pineapple, 94
  Spread, Nutty Carrot-
    Cheese, 50
Casseroles
  Burrito Supreme
    Casserole, 169
  Chicken and Pasta Bake, 191
  Chicken Tetrazzini, 118
  Green Bean and Artichoke
    Casserole, Italian, 139
  Grits and Sausage Casserole,
    Country, 39
  Ham and Broccoli Bake,
    Brunch, 39
  Ham and Potatoes,
    Scalloped, 68
  Ham and Spaghetti
    Casserole, 193
  Lasagna, 71
  Macaroni and Cheese,
    Old-Fashioned, 173
  New Potato Casserole, 189
  Potato Casserole, Hash
    Brown, 43
  Seafood Casserole, Royal, 220
  Tuna-Noodle Casserole,
    Favorite, 123
  Turkey and Wild Rice
    Casserole, 119
  Turkey Tortilla Casserole, 79
  Vegetable Combo,
    Curried, 143
Cheese. See also
  Appetizers/Cheese.
  Bread, Cottage
    Cheese-Dill, 185
  Chicken Romano, 116

Dessert Cheese,
  Date-Nut, 152
Dressing, Spinach Salad with
  Blue Cheese, 190
Eggplant Parmesan, 71
Frosting, Cream Cheese, 149
Lasagna, 71
Macaroni and Cheese,
  Old-Fashioned, 173
Noodles Romanoff, 130
Rolls, Turkey and
  Cheese, 57
Salad, Two Bean and
  Cheese, 212
Sandwiches, Baked Ham and
  Swiss, 51
Sandwiches, Toasted Chicken
  and Swiss, 75
Spreads and Fillings
  Carrot-Cheese Spread,
    Nutty, 50
  Ham and Cheese Spread,
    Savory, 51
  Herbed Cheese
    Spread, 197
  Pimiento Cheese
    Spread, 49
  Pineapple-Cheese
    Spread, 54
Squares, Lemon Cheese, 151
Strata, Cheese and
  Asparagus, 206
Toasts, Pesto-Parmesan, 193
Cheesecakes. See
  Cakes/Cheesecakes.
Chicken
  Artichoke Bake, Company
    Chicken-, 114
  Baked Chicken Breasts,
    Spicy, 215
  Broth, Chicken, 21
  Curry, Chicken, 175
  Dijon Chicken, 178
  Divan, Overnight
    Chicken, 218
  Fettuccine, Chicken, 74
  Flautas with Avocado Sauce,
    Chicken, 74
  Orange-Herb Chicken, 113
  Pasta Bake, Chicken
    and, 191
  Pockets, Chicken, 51
  Pot Pies, Country
    Chicken, 116
  Puffs, Chicken Cocktail, 91
  Roast Chickens, Savory, 73
  Rolls, Fiesta Chicken, 114
  Romano, Chicken, 116

Photographers and Stylists

Photography by Ralph Anderson; styling by Kay E. Clarke.

Additional photography by Jim Bathie, pages 18, 22, 25, 28, 30, 33, 38, 41, 194, 201, 203, 225, 226, 229; additional styling by Virginia R. Cravens, pages 194, 201, 203, 225, 226, 229.